BANGKOK

By John Blofeld
and the Editors of Time-Life Books

Photographs by Philip Jones Griffiths

THE GREAT CITIES · TIME-LIFE BOOKS · AMSTERDAM

The Author: John Blofeld was born in London in 1913 but has spent most of his life in the Far East. In the 1930s he travelled throughout China, studying Buddhism and other religions; after the Second World War, he pursued this interest in Peking on a Chinese government scholarship. He settled in Bangkok in 1951 and has lived there ever since, teaching English literature at various universities, and for 12 years working as Chief Editor for the United Nations Economic Commission for Asia and the Far East. He has written a score of books on Asian cultural matters.

The Photographer: Philip Jones Griffiths, born in 1936 in Rhuddlan, Wales, practised pharmacy until he took up photography full-time in 1961. Since then, he has contributed to many American and British publications, including *Life, Look, Queen* and *The Sunday Times Magazine*. In 1966 he joined the international photo agency, Magnum. He covered the Vietnam War for three years and in 1971 published his photographic reports as a book, *Vietnam Inc.*

WORLD WAR II
THE SEAFARERS
THE TIME-LIFE BOOK OF BOATING
THE GOOD COOK
TECHNIQUES OF PHOTOGRAPHY
THE TIME-LIFE ENCYCLOPAEDIA
OF GARDENING
HUMAN BEHAVIOUR
THE GREAT CITIES
THE ART OF SEWING
THE OLD WEST
THE WORLD'S WILD PLACES
THE EMERGENCE OF MAN
LIFE LIBRARY OF PHOTOGRAPHY
TIME-LIFE LIBRARY OF ART
FOODS OF THE WORLD
GREAT AGES OF MAN
LIFE SCIENCE LIBRARY
LIFE NATURE LIBRARY
YOUNG READERS LIBRARY
LIFE WORLD LIBRARY

TIME-LIFE INTERNATIONAL
EUROPEAN EDITOR: George Constable
Assistant European Editor: Kit van Tulleken
Design Director: Louis Klein
Chief Designer: Graham Davis
Director of Photography: Pamela Marke
Chief of Research: Vanessa Kramer
Chief Sub-Editor: Ilse Gray

THE GREAT CITIES
Series Editor: Simon Rigge
Editorial Staff for *Bangkok*
Deputy Editor: Christopher Farman
Designers: Joyce Mason, Derek Copsey
Picture Editor: Gunn Brinson
Staff Writers: Mike Brown, Tony Masters
Text Researchers: Jackie Matthews, Krystyna Davidson, Elizabeth Loving
Sub-Editor: Nicoletta Flessati

Editorial Production
Production Editor: Ellen Brush
Quality Control: Don Fragale
Traffic Co-Ordinators: Pat Boag, Joanne Holland
Art Department: Julia West
Editorial Department: Ajaib Singh Gill
Picture Department: Catherine Lewes, Stephanie Lindsay

The captions and the texts accompanying the photographs in this volume were prepared by the editors of TIME-LIFE Books.

Valuable assistance was given in the preparation of this volume by TIME-LIFE Correspondent David L. Terry, Bangkok.

Published by TIME-LIFE International (Nederland) B.V. Ottho Heldringstraat 5, Amsterdam 1018.

© 1979 TIME-LIFE International (Nederland) B.V. All rights reserved. First printing in English.

Cover: At Wat Arun, Bangkok's Temple of the Dawn, the moon god Pra Chan—identified by the white horse he bestrides—surveys his mortal subjects from a niche lavishly decorated with porcelain mosaic. In a city that has been rapidly adapted to a Westernized way of life, the many Buddhist temples with their eclectic array of deities preserve a strong sense of Thai tradition.

First end paper: An inlay of shimmering mother-of-pearl creates the illusion of perpetual moonlight playing on the strange forms of two *kinnari*—mythological beings who are part human, part bird—that decorates a door of Wat Rajabopitr, one of Bangkok's finest temples.

Last end paper: Gaudy primary colours—red, yellow and blue—provide a glowing background for pictures of pop singers, film stars and other Thai celebrities emblazoned on the covers of magazines at a Bangkok news-stand.

Contents

1

A Kingly Creation

It is strange how often a man's more fateful decisions seem to owe so much to chance and so little to design. Certainly chance ruled my coming to Bangkok—or Krungthep, "City of Deities", as the Thais call it. For many years I had been living and working in China as a student of Buddhism. Driven from my Peking home by the red tide of Mao's revolution in 1949, I left for Hong Kong with no thought of Thailand in my head. I knew little of the country except that it was no longer called Siam and that, judging from the few Thais I had met, its inhabitants were a friendly and attractive people with a positive zest for merriment and laughter. But while in Hong Kong I was offered a post as a teacher of English literature at Chulalongkorn University in Bangkok; and so, in 1951, I moved into a cultural milieu where *nagas* and *garudas*—the mythical serpent deities and bird-man progenitors of the South-East Asian peoples—displace Chinese dragons as the traditional upholders of divine order.

I soon felt at home in Bangkok, but I did not dream that I should still be here so many years later. Were someone to ask why I have stayed so long, I should be at a loss for a simple reply. The immediate attractions of the city are obvious enough: dazzling sunshine and lush tropical vegetation; ornate royal palaces; glittering Buddhist temples with snowy white or gilded spires; innumerable restaurants serving excellent food; and a night-life that has given the city a not altogether flattering reputation as the "Paris of the East". Of more lasting fascination is Bangkok's role as capital of the only country in South-East Asia never to have succumbed to European colonialism. In this city where kings reigned with absolute powers until earlier this century (and still possess great influence as constitutional monarchs), one can observe a way of life that has grown and evolved without major interruption since the far distant past.

Founded in 1782 and of no great size until its rapid expansion in the last few decades, Thailand's capital is now a busy, mostly modern conurbation of 4.5 million people—at least 40 times larger than the country's next biggest city, Chiang Mai, in the far north. Bangkok also has a disproportionate share of the nation's political, administrative, cultural, commercial and industrial institutions; and so it may be likened to an enormous head balanced upon an attenuated body.

The sprawl of the city is caught up in a loop of the Chao Phya River, formed where that majestic waterway, after flowing southwards through the lush rice-fields of the country's heartland, suddenly turns to the east before flooding south again to the Gulf of Thailand 25 miles away.

The bustling Chao Phya River winds through Bangkok, connecting the city with rice-growing areas to the north, and the Gulf of Thailand 25 miles south.

Because the land is flat and there are few multi-storey buildings, a bird's-eye view can be had from any modest vantage point. The scene is hardly exotic, apart from patches of tropical green and the curving river with its trains of rice-barges and swarms of small craft paddling in from rural areas. One looks out in every direction over street upon street of cement-coated, three- or four-storeyed brick buildings, varied by occasional modern office or apartment blocks. Teak, used to build much of the original Bangkok, is expensive these days and cheaper woods last barely 20 years in the hot, humid climate. Architectural tradition survives mainly in the scattering of temples and a few public buildings that incorporate such characteristically Thai features as cloister-like verandahs and roofs rising tier upon tier, agleam with colourful porcelain tiles.

Coming down into the streets, one is plunged at once into the city's appalling traffic congestion, which has been only slightly relieved in recent years by the construction of more and more overpasses at large inter-sections. The stream of lorries, buses, private cars, motor cycles and motorized trishaws (a three-wheeled variation on the rickshaw) on every street is so dense that progress is often slower than in the days when flat-bottomed boats plying the city's once-extensive network of *klongs*, or canals, were the normal means of transport. Klongs are still important thoroughfares in the district of Thonburi, on the western side of the river; but on the east side most of them have been filled in to provide more space for roads, or are being replaced by huge drainpipes able to take the run-off from the 45 inches of rain that fall on average each year.

There is no real central area in Bangkok, nothing remotely resembling the fashionable districts of London or Paris. Sumptuous hotels, well-appointed cinemas, modern office blocks and new shopping centres cluster here and there; but often they stand cheek by jowl with rows of modest shop-houses—family concerns with living quarters above them. The majority of shops are run by Chinese, or people of Chinese origin, who form the largest minority group in the city. These shops almost always look attractive, for Chinese merchants have a positive genius for window displays and for arranging goods so that any item comes to hand at a moment's notice. Increasingly, small air-conditioners are seen at the upper windows of relatively humble buildings and television aerials sprout on the roofs. Every few yards one comes upon a café or small restaurant; and there are plenty of hawkers selling sweetmeats, tropical fruit and—for the many thousands of tourists who pass through each year—orchids.

Most inhabitants of Bangkok dress informally in European-style clothes —open-collared shirt and trousers for men, and a thin dress or a blouse with a short skirt for women. Traditional *panungs*, shaped like huge sarongs but drawn up between the legs so that they resembled Indian dhotis, were worn almost universally by both men and women until 1941. In that year the Prime Minister, Marshal Phibul, banned indigenous dress;

he wanted the Thais to appear smart and up to date so that they would not be sneered at by the Japanese "allies" who had overrun the country. The change to modern clothes has survived because trousers and short skirts, besides being cheap, are better adapted to the exigencies of modern life. Another of Phibul's innovations has also endured: it was he who, in 1939, altered the country's name from Siam—a term of Chinese origin—to Thailand, meaning "Land of the Free".

Visitors may be forgiven if they feel that the Thais have turned their backs on the past and that Bangkok is just another Western-style city not easily distinguishable from modern cities elsewhere. But the Westerniz-ation is more apparent than real, as a fashionable housewife once made clear to me when I rashly voiced a contrary opinion. We were drinking lime juice on the lawn of her small but handsome villa off Sukhumvit Road in east Bangkok, a home where scarcely anything Thai was to be found, apart from the people who lived there, the food being prepared in the kitchen and a small Buddhist shrine-room on the upper floor.

"Really, Professor," she said, "you must get to know us better. Don't judge by externals, but by how we fit them into our lives and by what we are in ourselves. Is Thai poetry the less Thai for being printed in modern type? I noticed you eyeing my modern living-room furniture without approval, as though you would have us live like our ancestors, with no furniture to speak of beyond a few lacquered cabinets for books and knick-knacks, some foot-high tables for eating at while seated on the floor, and some rolled-up sleeping mats to be brought out at bedtime. Do you *farang* (Westerners) think it reasonable that we should abjure progress so that you can enjoy Bangkok like a museum? The truth is that Thais are Thais, however foreignized we may seem. I always think of us as being like those Siamese cats in the Disney film who sang: 'We are Siamese, if you please. We are Siamese, if you don't please!'"

She might have gone further, I now feel, by arguing that the Westernized clothes, furniture, architecture and mechanical gadgets to be seen everywhere in Bangkok are themselves an expression of two notable Thai characteristics: a love of novelty and an immense adaptability. And the Thais' traditional attitudes remain deeply ingrained: their easy-going, hedonistic approach to life; their kindness and tolerance; their dislike of extremes (which does not, however, preclude explosions of passion); their adherence to the Buddhist religion, with its emphasis on forbearance in the face of suffering and misfortune; and their spontaneous courtesy—to which the influence of centuries of rule by a monarchy considered divine has added an appealing degree of formality.

The Thais were originally one of the non-Chinese races (though not strikingly different from the Chinese in appearance) who dwelt in south-west China, where many still remain. Beginning in the 9th Century, they

Crowned by a gilded reliquary tower said to house some teeth of the Buddha, the so-called Golden Mount looms 250 feet above surrounding canal-side homes. The mount, artificially created with earth-fill and masonry on the flat swampland of Bangkok, replicates a sacred hilltop temple in the former Thai capital of Ayutthaya, razed by Burmese invaders in 1767.

began to migrate south-west from their homeland under the pressure of Chinese expansionism. Over the next 500 years, they settled in the fertile Chao Phya Valley and neighbouring areas of south-eastern Asia: the eastern part of present-day Burma; Assam in easternmost India; Laos; and parts of Vietnam. In all these regions varieties of Thai are spoken to this day.

The Thais of the Chao Phya Valley found other civilizations already established—chiefly the Khmers, whose empire lay mostly to the east, with Angkor as its capital, and whose descendants are the present-day Cambodians. At first, the small kingdoms set up by the incoming Thais were subject to Khmer overlordship; but in 1238 a powerful Thai warrior chief named Phra Ruang defeated the Khmers at their northern capital of Sukhothai in what is now north Thailand. He went on to establish the first independent Thai kingdom, centred on Sukhothai, and for more than a century it remained the greatest Thai power in the Chao Phya Valley. Nevertheless, Sukhothai never grew beyond a city-state. Its kings had influence over large areas of the surrounding countryside, but the life of the kingdom—politics, trade, administration—went on mostly within the protective walls of the city. This sharp distinction between town and country would be repeated in later Thai capitals, including Bangkok.

It was during the ascendancy of Sukhothai that the Thais embraced Buddhism, introduced by Indian missionaries and traders. But around 1350, Sukhothai was eclipsed by the rival Thai city-state of Ayutthaya, which retained its hegemony for 417 years. During the Ayutthaya period, Thai civilization became a distinctive blend of Chinese, Indian and Cambodian ingredients, with a sprinkling of elements from the Malay countries and from Persia. Buddhism remained the established religion; but Hindu gods and rituals were incorporated into the life of the kingdom, and Brahman priests—the highest caste of Hinduism—were installed at court to act as astrologers and to officiate at state ceremonies.

Perhaps the most spectacular of these was the annual Swinging Ceremony, performed to entertain the god Shiva who, in traditional Thai belief, comes down to this world and stays for 10 days in the first or second month of the year. The ceremony survived into modern times, and one of the most incongruous sights in Bangkok is the Giant Swing, 80 feet high, that still overshadows traffic pouring through the square of that name. Every year until the ceremony was abandoned in 1932, Shiva, impersonated by a nobleman, used to watch from a white pavilion as four-man teams of court Brahmans swung through an arc of 180°, soaring high above the city's roof-tops, and snatched purses from the top of a slender bamboo pole erected to the west of the swing. If successful, they won applause, but any untoward incident was regarded as a bad omen.

Ayutthaya, built on an island in the Chao Phya River, must have been an entrancing city. With its many gilded palaces and temples, its water-borne markets and miles of klongs, it astonished even the ambassadors sent from Versailles by Louis XIV in the 17th Century. Their reports were filled with stories of royal panoply, solid gold Buddha statues encrusted with jewels, courtiers and citizenry everywhere prostrate in worship of the king, and the busy river traffic, graced by regal gilt barges, of this island-city. Since the 16th Century, however, Thailand had been intermittently at war with Burma; and when the Burmese invaded Ayutthaya in 1767, they razed it to the ground, slaughtered or enslaved all but 10,000 of its one million inhabitants and killed the king.

The monarchy was quickly restored, however. One of the most successful and ambitious Thai generals, Taksin, had escaped from Ayutthaya. He rallied an army, chased the Burmese from the kingdom within a year and set up a third Thai capital downstream at Thonburi, just across the river from what was then the small fishing and trading village of Bangkok.

Thonburi is now an unprepossessing industrial suburb of Bangkok and nothing remains of Taksin's city apart from some crumbling fortress walls and Wat Arun, the magnificent Temple of the Dawn, completed in 1842. Its tall *prang*, or round-topped spire, rises close to the river and can be seen from many parts of Bangkok. Supported on the backs of guardians of faith, depicted as demons converted from evil by the Buddha's gentle doctrine, it is decorated all over with curious mosaic-work composed of tens of thousands of fragments of porcelain. When the temple was nearing completion, the supply of these fragments petered out and the people were asked to help. They gladly smashed their household porcelain and handed over the pieces, for by doing so they were "making merit" —performing a good deed that, according to Buddhist belief, would weigh in their favour in future lives.

Shortly after Wat Arun was begun, Taksin became mad. In 1782, he was deposed in a palace coup and clubbed to death (the shedding of blood was forbidden in royal executions). The throne was offered to another general, Chakri, who had secured his popularity a few years before by conquering the Lao capital of Vientiane and bringing back one of the most revered Thai images, a little 23-inch figure known as the Emerald Buddha, which had been lost to the Thais for more than two centuries. Chakri—later called Rama I, after a Hindu deity worshipped as the exemplar of chivalry and virtue—founded a dynasty that has lasted to this day; the throne is now occupied by Rama IX, better known as King Bhumibol Adulyadej.

The first decision of Rama I was to move the capital across the river to Bangkok. This was a strategic move, since Bangkok was well protected by water on one side and by a vast, swampy plain stretching away to east and south on the other. It was also a symbolic move, intended as a fresh and auspicious start for the kingdom.

The name Bangkok—which means "Village of the Wild Plums"— clearly would not do for a royal capital, and Rama I endowed it with a prodigious string of titles that had to be written or spoken in full during the

At the entrance to the Grand Palace, a Royal Thai Army notice warns visitors about the rules of dress in this revered area. Some startling instructions on the right have acquired unintended meanings through the translator's failure to include a negative.

transaction of official business: "City of Deities [Krungthep]; the Great City; the Residence of the Emerald Buddha; the Impregnable City of the God Indra; the Grand Capital of the World Endowed with Nine Precious Gems; the Happy City, Abounding in Enormous Palaces that Resemble the Heavenly Abode where Reigns the Reincarnated God; a City Given by Indra and Built by Vishnukarm." To Thais, Bangkok has been Krungthep ever since. Only foreigners have "rather arrogantly", as a scholarly old Thai gentleman once put it to me, "persisted in calling it by the name of that wretched village".

As befits a city founded by a king, the most splendid part of Bangkok is Rama I's Grand Palace, which stands close to the bank in the westernmost part of the river's loop. Actually it is not so much a palace as a city within a city. The palace compound, fortified by crenellated walls, covers one square mile and encloses spacious lawns as well as Bangkok's finest temple, Wat Phra Keo, the Temple of the Emerald Buddha. In the dim light of the interior, high on a gilded altar with a royal, nine-tiered ceremonial umbrella behind and crystal balls to either side representing the sun and moon, reposes the image—actually green jade not emerald— for which Rama I built the temple.

Thailand's year has three seasons, and at the start of each one the present King—like his predecessors—comes to Wat Phra Keo to change the Buddha's ceremonial robes: a gilt robe flecked with blue for the rainy season, from June to October; a long robe of solid gold for the cool season, from November to February; and a golden, diamond-studded tunic for the hot season, from March to May. These are some of the most important religious ceremonies of the Thai calendar. The Emerald

Morning crowds stream through east Bangkok. Since the city lacks adequate public transport facilities, its sidewalks and streets are chronically congested.

Buddha is uniquely bound up with the fate of the nation; for a Thai to swear by it is the equivalent of a Christian taking the oath on the Bible.

The Grand Palace complex, with its gorgeously coloured roofs and spires, is reminiscent of Moscow's Kremlin and Peking's fabulous Forbidden City. It is seen at its best if approached from the north-east when the skies are stained by the splendours of a tropical sunset. As one rounds a bend in Rajadamnoen Avenue—Bangkok's grandest boulevard, also known as the Way of Kings—the eye is met by a vista of battlemented walls stretching along two sides of the palace compound, the roofs and spires rising above them and sparkling in the slanting sunlight. Contemplating the Grand Palace at times like these, it is easy to visualize it as the centre from which the godlike powers wielded by generations of Thai monarchs radiated through cities, rice-fields, forests and mountains to the uttermost confines of the kingdom.

Within the grim outer wall of the palace were the king's council chamber and treasury, together with ministry buildings, a school, art studios, barracks for regiments of guards and artillery, and stables for horses and elephants. Within another set of walls was the inner palace, a fairyland of intricately carved wood, elaborate mosaic floors, mother-of-pearl designs on doors and panels, ornamental trees in china tubs, and heavily carved and gilded furniture on which rested ritual utensils of solid gold. The only males allowed in this inner sanctum were the king himself and sons who had not yet attained puberty. But there were three or four thousand women: scores of royal consorts, a great number of attendants and servants, female administrators, female functionaries, and even female police to keep order in the palace.

During the mid-19th-Century reign of King Mongkut (Rama IV), this was the court scene critically depicted by the widowed Mrs. Anna Leonowens, who helped educate the King's children and later acquired fame by writing two inaccurate books of memoirs, *The English Governess at the Siamese Court*, published in 1870, and *Siamese Harem Life*, which appeared three years later. The two volumes provided source material for Margaret Landon's novel *Anna and the King of Siam*, published in 1945; and this work in turn became the basis of the 1951 musical *The King and I*, by Richard Rodgers and Oscar Hammerstein. Although by European standards there was indeed something exotic about King Mongkut's 32 wives and 82 children—he was the most progenitive of the Chakri monarchs—*The King and I* was a monstrous edifice of romantic fiction erected on shaky foundations, interesting only because it has received such attention worldwide.

In 1932, the monarchy was shorn of its absolute powers in a bloodless coup that was supposed to open the way for a democratic system of government, but in fact inaugurated a series of army dictatorships interspersed with only brief democratic interludes. The Grand Palace, once so crowded with people, has become a rather silent, empty place since the present King moved to the more modern Chitralada Palace in north Bangkok soon after his accession in 1946. Nowadays, the old palace is used only for state banquets and other formal occasions, although the presence of the revered Emerald Buddha within its precincts ensures that it remains much more than a museum.

It is also regarded as the hub of the city. Bangkok, like Ayutthaya before it, took shape as a fortified city tightly enclosing the royal palace. The landward approaches on the east were secured by two klongs dug in concentric arcs; the outer one was made more difficult to cross by a high wall along its edge, and later a third klong was added, with new fortifications. Within this island stronghold lived civil servants and their families, as well as professional men. Merchants had to live outside the walls, since theirs was considered an inferior calling.

Today, many ministries of the Thai government are still housed within the old city. Bangkok's most gorgeous temples and revered shrines are here as well. Just north of the Grand Palace is a large open space known as the Pramane Ground, or Sanam Luang; it is used regularly for weekend markets and also, more notably, for royal cremations. On the east side of the grounds is the small shrine known as Lak Muang, "The Pillar of the City"—a nine-foot-high carved wooden pillar erected by Rama I to house Bangkok's guardian deity. Lak Muang is believed to have the power to bring good fortune to those who offer flowers and incense. Petitioners whose wishes come true tie brightly coloured scarves around the pillar or put on concerts or plays in the courtyard outside the shrine.

The city began to lose its medieval, water-borne character during the reign of King Mongkut. In 1860, he converted an old elephant trail leading out of the city into New Road, the first thoroughfare in Bangkok suitable for wheeled traffic. Starting close to the Grand Palace, New Road runs south-east and then south along the curve of the river to the old European sector, which is still punctuated with a few remaining embassies and the Oriental Hotel, once almost as grand as Raffles in Singapore or Shepheards in Cairo. Many people thought at the time that the King had built the road in order to have somewhere to drive his new horse carriages. In fact, he recognized that wheeled vehicles were essential to commercial expansion and the rapid growth of that part of the city proved his point. Though rather down at heel nowadays, it is still a very lively commercial district.

Rajadamnoen Avenue, the Way of Kings, was another pioneering road. Built by Mongkut's successor, King Chulalongkorn (Rama V), it cuts a broad swathe east from the vicinity of the Grand Palace and then turns north. Chulalongkorn had visited Europe in the 1890s and wanted a majestic avenue of his own to rival those of London and Paris. Bordered now by banks and offices, it ends at the Royal Plaza—embellished with an equestrian statue of Chulalongkorn—and is used for major spectacles

High-rises in downtown Bangkok tower above the graceful roofs of a 19th-Century temple, while an oil refinery in the distance holds aloft a sky-staining torch.

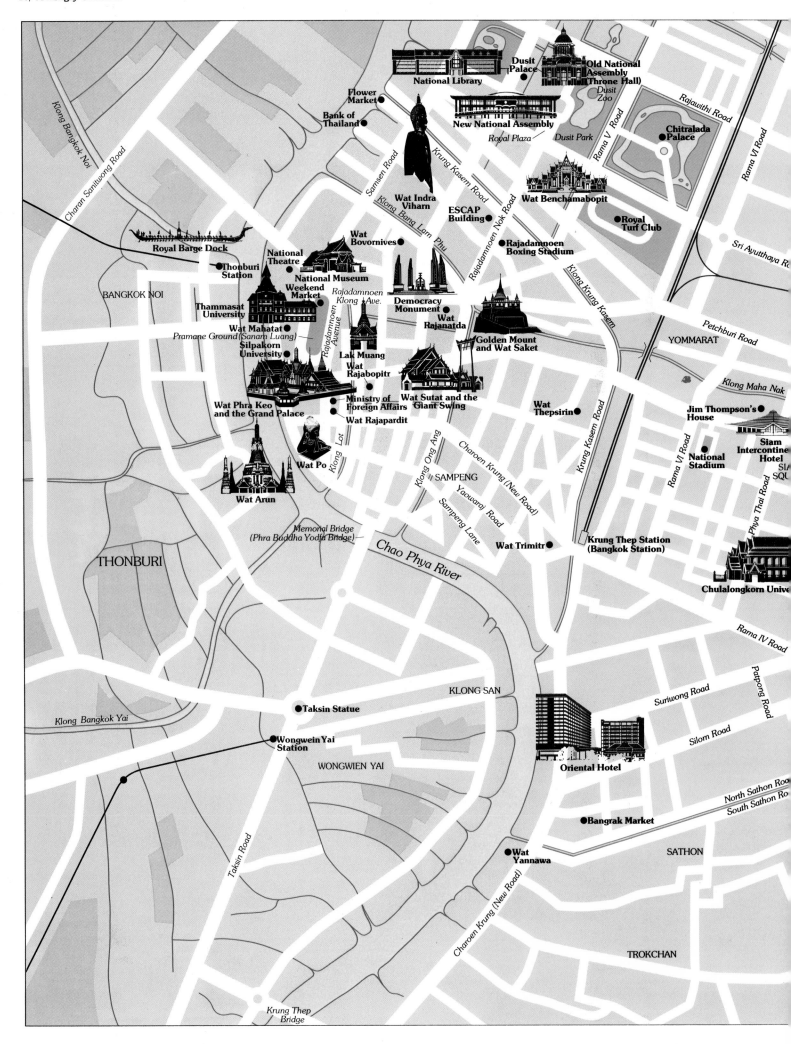

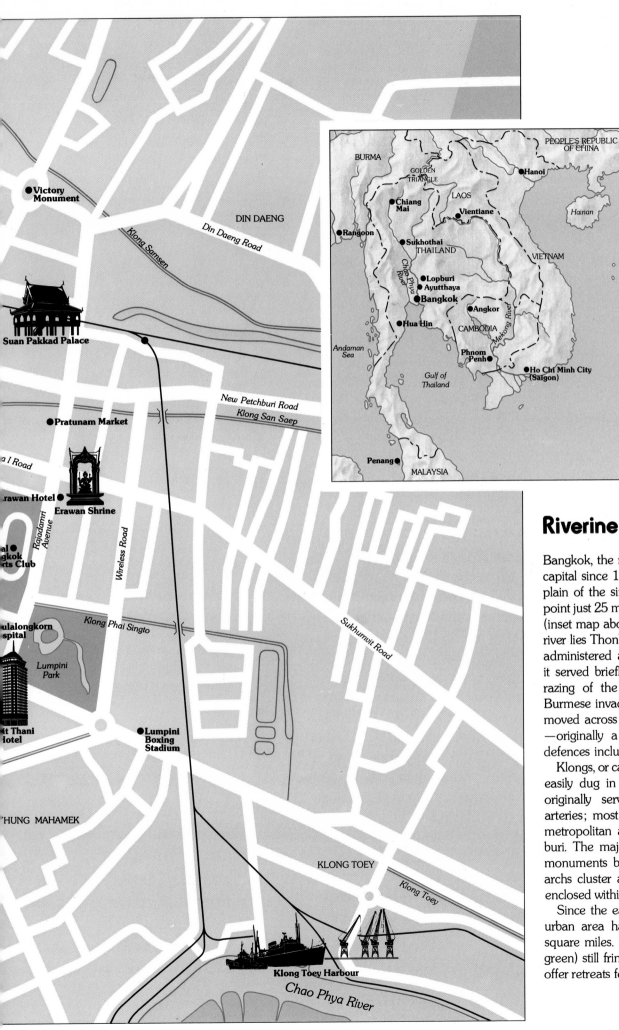

Victory
Monument

DIN DAENG

Din Daeng Road

Klong Samsen

Suan Pakkad Palace

New Petchburi Road
Klong San Saep

Pratunam Market

...a I Road

...awan Hotel
Erawan Shrine

Rajadamri Avenue

Wireless Road

...al
...gkok
...ts Club

Klong Phai Singto

...ulalongkorn
...spital

Lumpini
Park

Sukhumvit Road

...t Thani
...otel

Lumpini
Boxing
Stadium

...HUNG MAHAMEK

KLONG TOEY

Klong Toey

Klong Toey Harbour

Chao Phya River

PEOPLE'S REPUBLIC
OF CHINA

Kwangtung Province

Swatow

BURMA

GOLDEN
TRIANGLE

Macao
Hong Kong

Hanoi

Chiang
Mai

LAOS

Vientiane

Hainan

Rangoon

Sukhothai
THAILAND

Chao Phya River

VIETNAM

*South China
Sea*

Lopburi
Ayutthaya
Bangkok

Angkor

Mekong River

Hua Hin

CAMBODIA

*Andaman
Sea*

Phnom
Penh

Ho Chi Minh City
(Saigon)

Palawan

*Gulf of
Thailand*

Penang

MALAYSIA

BORNEO

Riverine Sprawl

Bangkok, the main port of Thailand and its capital since 1782, sprawls across the delta plain of the sinuous Chao Phya River at a point just 25 miles from the Gulf of Thailand (inset map above). On the west bank of the river lies Thonburi, a semi-rural municipality administered as part of Greater Bangkok; it served briefly as a Thai capital after the razing of the royal city of Ayutthaya by Burmese invaders in 1767. The capital was moved across the river to Bangkok proper —originally a fishing village—because its defences included a vast marsh to the east.

Klongs, or canals (blue on large map) were easily dug in the flat, alluvial terrain and originally served as the city's transport arteries; most of those that remain in the metropolitan area (fawn) criss-cross Thonburi. The major wats, palaces and historic monuments built by successive Thai monarchs cluster about the city's oldest sector, enclosed within a loop of the river.

Since the early 20th Century, Bangkok's urban area has increased from 5 to 115 square miles. But fields and orchards (light green) still fringe the city and parks (green) offer retreats for its 4.5 million people.

such as troop reviews and the annual ceremony when students and public servants honour the memory of the Thais' most modernizing monarch.

Under King Chulalongkorn, Bangkok became one of the largest and most prosperous cities in South-East Asia. The King initiated the building of so many other roads that, by the start of the 20th Century, more of the city's trade was being carried on land than by water. By 1908, some 300 motor vehicles were rattling along the new thoroughfares—a development encouraged no doubt by the King's own frequent excursions behind the wheel of his yellow electric car. Western-style architecture for the first time intruded on the temple-dominated skyline and north Bangkok became the leafy, spacious district it is today, with the modern Chitralada Palace, the Royal Turf Club racecourse and the gardens of Dusit Park at its centre.

Nevertheless, Bangkok's fastest growth came much later: in the 1950s and 1960s, the population mushroomed from 1.5 million to its present 4.5 million. Beyond the purlieus of royal north Bangkok, new middle-class villas and apartment houses, neither unattractive nor particularly inspiring, stretch out towards the international airport. To the east, a whole new commercial and residential area has grown up; smart restaurants, super-markets, hotels, furniture and tailoring shops line Sukhumvit Road, while sleazy nightclubs predominate along Petchburi Road.

The area beyond the old commercial district in the south-east was once notable for large private gardens with old trees, rice-fields and dense coconut plantations. But the advance of commerce and industry is relentless and not much remains here of the pleasant greenery that once characterized so much of the city. What is worse, the city has grown haphazardly, without careful planning or zoning, as I know to my cost. Nearly 20 years ago I remarked to a member of the royal family, whom I used to know, that I was taken by the beauty of the traditional-style wooden buildings at his seaside estate close to the Gulf of Thailand. "Well," he said, "you could easily have the same kind of house in Bangkok. It has always been the custom to make them in sections so that they are easy to transport. Prefabricated housing may well be a Thai invention." The upshot was that he had a house constructed for me and sent, in sections, to Bangkok.

In readiness, I had bought a small piece of land in an open field scheduled for development in what was to become a middle-class residential area along Sukhumvit Road. The house, when it rose, over-looked a shallow lake covered with water-iris. My living-quarters, raised 10 feet above the ground on stout wooden pillars as a defence against floods, consist of three parallel sections, each with a handsomely pointed roof supported on tiers of beams. Huge planks of darkly gleaming teak compose the floor; and the inner and outer walls are built of a wood that is cheaper than teak but still hard enough to resist the onslaughts of insects, sun and rain. It is actually a simple dwelling, but lovely in its way.

Alas, when other buildings arose about it, my new neighbours proved

With a bagful of paper wrappings at the ready, a boy roams through the streets of Bangkok selling jasmine blossom garlands from a tray. The fragrant garlands are associated with good fortune and may be presented to friends as gifts, left at temples as offerings—or simply kept by the purchaser to foster luck.

indifferent to Bangkok's sketchy zoning regulations. Instead of being surrounded by other villas, I have a five-storey printing works just a few feet from my windows to the east; this building not only generates a thumping noise by day and night, but has plunged the rooms on that side into perpetual gloom and cut off my garden from the minimum amount of sunshine needed by flowering shrubs. To the west now stands a radio repair factory, blaring forth a cacophony of programmes throughout the day. Worst of all, opposite my front gate is an overnight parking area for a score of large trucks; revving up from 5.30 a.m. onwards, they produce an hour-long sequence of shattering din.

This sort of helter-skelter development is all too familiar in Bangkok. To give just one other example, I know of a Buddhist monastery that now lies next to a poultry market. The squawking of doomed birds, the shouts of vendors and the roar of traffic from the nearby main street must constitute such an obstacle to meditative equanimity as to arouse, even in saintly breasts, the very passions the monastic life is intended to subdue.

The rapid growth of the city in the last 20 to 30 years has produced slums and overcrowding, though nothing to match the poverty and suffering of cities in India, Pakistan or Bangladesh. Two large slums disfigure the northern outskirts of the city and the Klong Toey harbour area. They consist of poorly constructed single-storey wooden dwellings largely devoid of furniture and lacking proper drainage, though a good number of the houses are incongruously surmounted by television aerials. To combat the growth of these shanty towns, the government has put up many five- or

The colossal toe-nails (below) of a Buddha that stands 108 feet high outside the monastic complex of Wat Indra Viharn in central Bangkok make perfect altars for offerings of gold leaf, flowers and incense. The full statue (inset)—made of cement, with gold-painted hair and tiny gold tiles on the face—is backed by a spire-topped white tower that offers visitors a panorama of the city.

six-storey concrete blocks of flats; though they are far from beautiful, at least they have electricity, running water and adequate drainage. But impoverished rural families are pouring into the city far faster than public housing can be built to accommodate them.

Fortunately, Thais, like most Asians, are accustomed to living at close quarters. Young factory workers feel it no great hardship to sleep in dormitories provided by their employers; and among the poor, newly married couples are generally content to rent a single, barely furnished room. Many families happily take their meals seated cross-legged on the floor, in the old manner—though they would not be averse to tables and chairs if these could be purchased without sacrificing the television set.

Closely connected with poverty and rural migration is crime, which has been alarmingly on the increase. Many newcomers, cut off from the traditions that for centuries gave meaning to the lives of their ancestors in far-off villages, are disorientated by their move to the city. Most of the criminals convicted of robbery, drug pushing, rape or murder come from this sort of background. The girls tend to take to prostitution, and their male counterparts to pimping, confidence tricks, pickpocketing and general thuggery.

Civil unrest of a more formal kind has been rare in Bangkok, in spite of the *coups d'état* and army dictatorships that followed the end of royal absolutism in 1932. When I first came to Bangkok, Thailand was a strikingly peaceful country, and although the international environment looked increasingly hostile after the Communist takeover in China, there were no severe internal problems. Coups rarely caused much bloodshed and few of the military regimes aroused widespread resentment. In 1973, however, the mostly moderate pattern of Thai politics was startlingly disrupted. The military regime, its image already tarnished by its support of the interventionist Asian policy then being pursued by the United States, was strongly criticized by the students and intelligentsia, who demanded a democratic constitution and social reforms. Unwisely, the government arrested some key intellectuals in the constitutional reform movement.

This arbitrary action, no doubt prompted by fears that Communist agents were playing on left-wing idealism, mobilized the students, hitherto remarkable for their lack of political involvement. Massive demonstrations were held in Bangkok and one huge rally on October 14 was fired on by police and troops. About 90 demonstrators were killed. At the height of the crisis, the government fell, to be replaced by a caretaker administration led by the Rector of Thammasat University, Professor Sanya Thammasakdi, who promised a new constitution and elections.

Democratic politics were soon demonstrated to be less than satisfactory. Elections in 1975 produced an unstable coalition government drawn from some of the 22 parties that held seats in the National Assembly. (No less than 42 parties had contended for these seats.) Although the government's

A bleak public housing project (below) nearing completion in Bangkok's crowded port area faces the same fate as a neighbouring apartment block (right): television aerials and laundry sprouting from the windows, grounds littered with refuse. Such low-cost units fall far short of meeting the housing needs of the thousands who flood into Bangkok each year from rural areas, and shanty towns continue to mar the city.

intentions were good, its concern to avoid authoritarian tactics encouraged disrespect for the law. Demonstrations, strikes and a series of political murders followed, and even the Prime Minister's house was looted. At the same time, with the end of the Vietnam War, the fall of Saigon, and the installation of Communist regimes there as well as in Cambodia and Laos, Thailand had much to fear from across its borders.

Leftist groups, infiltrated by Communists, organized big demonstrations; and right-wing organizations with names like the Red Bulls were hastily formed to defend traditional values. A youth movement known as the Village Scouts, established with royal blessing in 1971 for the ostensible purpose of providing community service, was taken in hand by army officers and developed into a paramilitary strike force.

In October 1976, polarization in politics culminated in horrifying bloodshed. Fears of a right-wing coup encouraged left-wing students at Thammasat University to stage a huge rally on October 4. They also put on a skit in which two of their number played the parts of union leaders who had been lynched by police a few weeks earlier in north-east Thailand. The skit ended with a simulated hanging. One of the victims had been made up in such a way that he bore a marked resemblance to the King's son, Crown Prince Vajiralongkorn. Though the suggestion was claimed to be accidental, it was nevertheless taken by many Thais as lese-majesty, a crime carrying a penalty of seven years' imprisonment.

Reports of the incident were broadcast over the armoured division radio station, which reflected extreme right-wing opinion, and the next day an angry mob besieged the Thammasat campus. Early on October 6, fighting broke out between the two sides. Paramilitary police, Village Scouts and other vigilantes carrying heavy weapons, metal bars, knives and sticks invaded the campus, killing 46 students and wounding nearly 200. Fighting continued all morning, by which time more than 2,000 students had been arrested. A further thousand were jailed before the week was out.

To this day, opinions vary as to who fired the first shot. Blame for what happened has been attributed to groups ranging from the illegal Communist Party of Thailand to the CIA and right-wing *agents provocateurs*. In any case, a military junta seized power, declared martial law, and dissolved parliament and all political parties. Although most of the arrested students were soon released and all charges of subversion or lese-majesty were eventually dropped, more than a thousand student refugees fled to the jungles in the north-east or crossed into Laos and Cambodia, where they joined Communist insurgency movements whose activities continue to pose a threat to the security of Thailand.

When one considers the modern problems of Thailand, both internal and external, it is tempting to imagine the past as brighter and more perfect than it really was. However, that said, I must confess to a certain nostalgia

for Bangkok as it used to be some 20 years ago. The city then consisted mostly of low wooden houses surrounded by gardens, many of them with flowering shrubs and fruit-trees whose foliage glistened enchantingly after rain. My favourite plants were an exotic kind of palm shaped like a Chinese fan; scarlet hibiscus; frangipani with its glossy branches and lovely waxen flowers; and mango trees, worth cherishing for their beauty quite apart from their gloriously scented fruit. None of these plants are now rare, but one no longer sees vistas of them as in those days. Roads were much fewer and narrower than they are now and the surfaces were terrible, but I cannot forget the joy of driving for miles and never encountering a traffic jam—an impossibility today.

Now that so many of the old canals have vanished, there are fewer mosquitoes and other pests; snakes are rarely seen within the city limits, whereas in the past one seldom drove out anywhere without seeing the flattened corpses of snakes lying on the road. But it is sad that residents of the built-up areas are deprived of the nightly concerts in the gardens. The choirs consisted of frogs and insects singing before or after rain, the total volume of sound being as great as that of a radio turned full on—and infinitely more melodious to my ears than the general run of Thai and Western pop music. The booming and honking, chirruping and twittering seemed to be synchronized with a rhythm dictated by giant bullfrogs, whose voices would have done credit to the base section of a Russian choir. The music made by these creatures, for all its volume, was strangely soothing and encouraged rather than hindered sleep. Still, there are compensations for the loss of a more rural atmosphere, not the least of which are my air-conditioned bedroom and the knowledge that I can now take my choice of restaurants offering cuisines from all over the world, or buy almost any item of merchandise that West or East produce.

And of course, the climate has not changed. To a newcomer, the weather in Bangkok may seem oppressively hot and humid, but personally I would not exchange it for the damp chill of a northern winter, with its attendant coughs, colds, bronchitis and rheumatism. The city enjoys its finest weather during the so-called cool season, from November to February. Although the temperature can be over 80°F. at midday, there are periods of a week or so when icy winds from China, having lost their ferocity en route, arrive in Bangkok as delicious breezes, with perhaps enough nip in them to encourage young girls to wear flattering sweaters. The skies are usually cloudless and the humidity comparatively low. Towards the end of the cool season, one witnesses a strange phenomenon: the simultaneous arrival of spring and autumn. Evergreen plants now take on an intense greenness, while those that are deciduous burst into their finest autumnal colours.

Then suddenly the hot season is upon us. From March to May, the temperature rises at noon to around 97°F., if not higher, and seldom falls below 77°F. at night. This is the time for vacations and the school

Forewarned by darkening skies, stall-holders at a market near Wat Phra Keo hurry to pack up their goods before the onset of a monsoon shower in June.

Minutes later, the rain falls in such strength that the wat is blocked from view and vendors have to buttress their canopies. The downpour will last an hour or so.

calendar is arranged accordingly. Two of Thailand's most delicious fruits, the strange-smelling durian and the gloriously scented mango, ripen during these months. They are accompanied by a host of others—rambutan, looking like huge spiked strawberries; pure white mangosteen nestling in a scarlet bed surrounded by hard purplish skin; juicy pomelos, resembling giant grapefruit, but sweet instead of sour and with a delicate pinkish tinge to their flesh; the scarlet or deep-orange pawpaw, so sweet that it needs a few drops of lime juice to make it perfect; and, late in the season, the lichee and its smaller relative the "dragon's eye" (known locally as *lamyai*). With such an exotic cornucopia, one is apt to overlook the huge water-melons and honey-sweet pineapples that are plentiful at almost any time of the year.

During the rainy season from June to October, temperatures drop a few degrees. Rain falls almost every day, but it comes in cataract-like downpours that are too brief to interfere much with one's routine; in any case, getting soaked to the skin is no great hardship in so warm a climate. Garments can safely be left to dry on one's body, which may take only 10 or 15 minutes, for sunshine follows swiftly. Most people in Bangkok enjoy the rain and one sees children running out to dance in it. Rainfall on important days, like weddings or birthdays, is thought highly auspicious. In gardens and orchards around the city, trees and plants grow by leaps and bounds. I have seen banana trees add inches to their height within a single week, such is the effect of the monsoon.

Long before Bangkok was saddled with the irreverent soubriquet "Paris of the East", it boasted another misleading guide-book title—the "Venice of the East", given on account of the many klongs that did service as streets. Now that so many of the city's klongs have been filled in, the only time Bangkok remotely resembles Venice is when floods are created by the combination of abnormal rainfall in the northern mountains at the source of the Chao Phya River, and high tides that force their way upriver from the sea. At such times—towards the end of the rainy season—Bangkok's streets are turned into waterways. Cars stall and motorists curse; but the city does take on a slightly Venetian appearance, as though hospitably trying to live up to its fictitious reputation for the benefit of guests.

Throughout the year, the few klongs that remain in the central areas of Bangkok are alive with motorized water-taxis which, though tiresomely noisy, travel at a speed that creates a cool, spray-laden wind. The more traditional, slower life of the klongs has almost disappeared except in Thonburi, on the west side of the river. Many canals still weave through that suburb, and their banks are lined with low wooden dwellings and small temples interspersed with greenery. Most houses have steps leading down to the water and the inhabitants spend so much time bathing, washing clothes or visiting one another in boats that they seem almost aquatic.

Sightseers are scarcely welcome on the Thonburi canals; the fast motor boats that transport them create waves that wash away the banks and endanger the small craft in which pedlars carry garden produce, cooked food and iced drinks from house to house. Hundreds of tourists are taken daily to see the so-called Floating Market on one of these canals; but the produce-laden boats that gave the market its name have largely vanished, so great is the disturbance caused by the tourist craft.

For a resident, the newer aspects of Bangkok, though often obtrusive, are not overwhelming. Old customs still play a considerable part in the lives of my Thai friends, and the pace of life in the city is still relatively unhurried. The ease of living in this hot, fertile land, which was comparatively underpopulated until modern times, has created among Thais an appreciation of leisure that is slow to change. Office hours are nominally from 8.30 a.m. to 4.30 p.m. five days a week; but the lunch hour is pleasantly elastic and people see no need to keep their noses diligently to the grindstone all the working day.

Buddhism, too, has played its part in moderating the outlook on life, creating an admirable equanimity. "The Buddha rightly taught that life is inseparable from suffering," a chubby businessman remarked to me after listening to an eloquent plea for modern efficiency techniques voiced by an ulcerous American associate. "We cannot escape the sorrows of bereavement, sickness, old age and death; but that is no reason for not having all the fun we can. It would be unforgivable to expect my staff to add to the tedium of their work by cutting out chit-chat, laughter and a little rest now and then to glance at the papers, or by driving out the vendors who bring them snacks and the many cooling drinks demanded by our climate. Who would opt for paradise on Saturdays and Sundays, or in old age, at the price of spending every working day in hell? I tell you, that man is joyless. Rich he may be, but did you notice how bald and thin, and how his smiles reach no further than his lips and teeth?"

While such attitudes may be responsible for many evils in Bangkok—noise and air pollution, haphazard development and all the inconveniences that go with it—the very lack of rigidity makes it possible to enjoy more freedom to be oneself than in societies where everything is carefully supervised. Provided people are discreet and decorous in their public conduct, there is a tolerance of human foibles, a beguiling "live and let live" atmosphere. The owner of the radio repair factory next to my house expects me to accept without complaint the noise necessarily made there during business hours, but he in his turn refrains from complaining that the boughs of my trees extend far into his yard and that my creepers are festooned on the wall of his building. Although Thailand is no longer a country with ample space for all, and though life is no longer so easy that little exertion is required beyond reaching out for bananas, mangoes and coconuts as they drop benevolently from the trees, something of the old carefree spirit lingers from those days.

Life on the Klongs

Travelling down a minor klong, a woman in a motorized canoe and an ice cream seller in a humbler craft pass children taking a dip by their roofed boat.

Beyond the bustle of central Bangkok, older, more subdued rhythms of life prevail on the hundreds of miles of canals—called *klongs* in Thai—that radiate from the broad Chao Phya River. Although most of the waterways on the east side of the river have been filled in to create roads, those in Thonburi and other districts to the west function much as they did when the city was laid out as a capital some 200 years ago. Klong-side dwellers, living in teak homes raised on stilts to guard against monsoon floods, use the waters for bathing, for washing dishes or laundry, and for sewage disposal—a grossly unhealthy system that relies on the tide as a natural flush. Above all, the klongs serve as arteries of transport, carrying craft that range from speedy water buses for commuters to sampans that deliver mail or sell all manner of snacks and other food.

Descending from their house into a klong, Thai children—one of them shorn in accord with a local religious custom—combine ablutions with a morning swim.

A burly klong-dweller's pet surrenders—with minimal grace—to a shampoo.

A young couple look on from a ladder perch as their breakfast eggs are fried in a floating cook-shop. The cook's reed-woven sun-hat is varnished against rain.

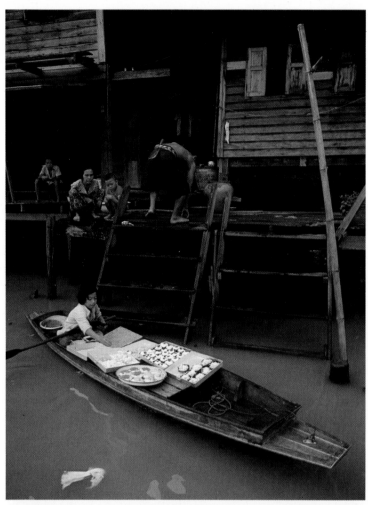

Arranged on a makeshift deck, trays of Thai cakes entice the sweet-toothed.

A grocery store owner receives the day's mail from the water-borne postman.

In a floating market, a woman (left) pays for her lunch, while a sampan packed with dark red rambutan fruit offers the prospect of a juicy dessert.

Packed to overflowing, a motor-powered canoe carries a load of hay up a sylvan klong. The hay will feed the buffalo that plough neighbouring paddy-fields.

Set back from the klong that brings its customers, a clothing store displays Western fashions—increasingly popular in Thailand—on a mannequin in the window.

Rocked by the wash of water buses carrying workers home, rice-barges ride low in the water of a broad Thonburi klong as they await off-loading at a warehouse.

Unable to use the motor at low tide, klong-travellers resort to muscle power.

In Bangkok's Samrong district, youngsters angle for edible fish in the shallow water of a klong that has become choked with weeds through lack of dredging.

2

The Hidden City

Beneath the brash, modern veneer of Bangkok, with its office blocks, shopping centres, nightclubs and traffic-choked streets, the continuance of old traditions can be seen in a thousand small but significant ways. One notices, for example, the citizens' personal gracefulness—a legacy, perhaps, of more spacious and unhurried days—and the sartorial elegance that even quite poor people achieve at small expense on festive occasions. Cleanliness and neatness in appearance are so highly esteemed that, even in the meanest backstreets, the sight of a truly unkempt or dirty person is rare. A painstaking artistry, too, goes into the preparation of food and into the immaculate floral decorations used in religious ceremonies. Even the educated classes—who, of all Bangkok's social strata, most resemble their American or European counterparts—retain essentially local ways of doing things. Not only do they speak Thai, eat Thai and think Thai, but they also arrange their lives in Thai fashion; that is to say, tradition plays an underlying part in most of their activities.

The most distinctive sign of this Thai culture is the formality that governs every aspect of people's lives, from the performance of family duties to business etiquette. Social life in Bangkok would be unimaginable without it. Even among close friends a relaxed, yet important, code of decorum sets the tone. Nevertheless, since Thais are probably the most polite race in the world (graciously polite, that is, without being servile), a visitor who transgresses the code is unlikely to receive any hint of his error, no matter how grave. I remember the misfortune that befell a newly appointed American ambassador to Thailand. Very properly, he decided that it would be courteous to call on the Supreme Patriarch, the highest Buddhist dignitary in the land. The local press at first lauded this gesture, then, a day or two later, published a photograph showing His Excellency seated comfortably in a chair, with his legs crossed in such a way that one foot pointed directly at the revered monk.

Unwittingly, the ambassador had committed an appalling social gaffe. Feet, as the lowest part of the body, are thought highly inelegant, and so from earliest youth a Thai is taught to be conscious of the offence to which careless postures may give rise. Above all, it is considered the height of bad manners to direct the toes or the soles of the feet at anyone—never mind a holy person. I wonder whether the ambassador's advisers told him what an adverse sensation this photograph caused throughout the city.

It would be rash to make this little story into a parable explaining the Western Powers' costly misunderstandings in their dealings with Asian

Western influence has been pervasive since Thailand opened its doors to foreign ideas in the middle of the 19th Century, but the Thais have nonetheless maintained a firm hold on traditional values in social behaviour, family life and public decorum.

A customer inspects one of the amulets on sale at a stall near Wat Mahatat in central Bangkok. Such charms, often representing the Buddha or revered kings and monks, are considered to be highly efficacious in promoting good luck and warding off danger. Although the principles of Buddhism oppose the wearing of amulets, most Thais possess at least one.

countries; but it is true that Europeans and Americans have traditionally underestimated the complexity of Asian society. To be understood—and to avoid being misunderstood—it is essential to learn the local rules.

Luckily, my years in pre-Communist China had warned me what to expect before I came to Thailand and I made a point, soon after my arrival, of asking about what was "done" and "not done". I put my question to a beautifully mannered young man named Khun Vichien ("Khun" is a courtesy title used where Westerners would say "Mr.", "Mrs." or "Miss"). At first he tried to dissuade me from worrying about such matters. With a cheerful *"Mae!"*—the Thai equivalent of "For heaven's sake!"—he told me that, as a foreigner and a guest, I had no need to bother: "Just be yourself, be comfortable, have a good time. That's all people will expect. It's not as though you were a Thai."

He eyed me mischievously, perhaps unconvinced that a large Englishman could ever acquire the grace with which Thai ceremonial gestures must be performed. But I insisted. "Then keep in mind these words," Khun Vichien said, "Noble head, ignoble feet."

After explaining how the feet are so liable to cause offence, he went on: "By tradition our heads are sacred, and not long ago even barbers used to apologize before laying hands on a customer's hair. You're not likely to go around patting people on the head, I know, but do remember to avoid letting any part of you pass above even a seated person's head. And never appear to stand over someone. Being tall, you are standing over me now; that doesn't matter because I'm much younger, so the rule doesn't apply. All the same, at formal gatherings, as you walk past people already seated, you should arch your body forward slightly. They'll be quite satisfied with the merest gesture—no need to walk around bent double!

"And of course," he went on, "you must also learn to *wai* correctly." The *wai* gesture, probably the first social act a Thai child learns, is the greeting customarily used when people in the West would shake hands. However, it is capable of refinements beyond the scope of the handshake and is also used when making an apology or when expressing thanks. To illustrate the gesture, Khun Vichien placed his hands palm to palm, with the tips of the fingers almost touching his nose. "That's where your hands should be for greeting equals. Bring them a good deal higher to show particular respect. You must never, never be the first to *wai* social inferiors, such as your students, servants, children or anyone much younger than yourself; but you must be careful to return their *wai*. You wait for them to *wai* and then you make the same gesture, only more casually and with the hands held lower down. It may seem undemocratic, but democracy is young here and, if you do not observe the rules, it would be much better not to *wai* at all."

Girls, I was to discover, know how to *wai* deliciously, sinking into a half or full curtsey, their bodies rippling like waves. But they only demonstrate that skill to show great respect—or maybe to catch the eye of an attractive male.

"Apart from learning to *wai* properly," Khun Vichien concluded, "I can think of only two rules of behaviour worth mentioning. The first is to avoid contradicting people or even voicing disagreement unless it is done with the greatest diffidence; the second is always to act as though perfectly at ease yourself. Then everyone will take you for a real Thai gentleman!"

Later I was to learn of more subtle forms of etiquette inherent in the Thai language. Less than in Japanese, but much more than in any European tongue, choice of vocabulary depends on the speaker's standing in relation to the person spoken to. Different sets of words apply to people of different status, rather as though we had to say in English that high dignitaries "partake of sustenance", that our equals "consume nourishment", and that juniors just "eat". There are four or five common ways of saying "I" and about the same number of alternatives for "you"—all implying shades of social status.

In polite conversation, one of two particles—*khrab* or *kha*—must terminate almost every sentence. They are among a number of Thai words expressing courtesy or respect. They cannot be directly translated, though both are close in mood to "Sir" or "Madam". Their use, perversely, is determined by the sex of the speaker, not that of the person addressed. Both terms may also be used to mean "yes", with complications that can spill over into English. For instance, Thais whose knowledge of English is poor sometimes say "yes" when they simply wish to convey respect: in other words, "Though I don't understand a thing you say, be sure that I am listening attentively!" A foreigner asking whether he can have eggs and bacon for breakfast may thus be disconcerted to find that the answer "yes" is followed by the arrival of rice porridge.

Even the citizens of Bangkok may sometimes be led astray by the word "yes", unless they are well schooled in all the refinements of its use. It is thought so improper to contradict flatly or to refuse a request outright that speakers often resort to deliberate vagueness. Consequently it may be hard to distinguish between positive and negative responses, and it becomes necessary to differentiate degrees of yes-ness ranging from "yes indeed" through "yes perhaps" to "yes not-at-all". Indications of the speaker's real intention have to be sought less in the words than in nuances of tone or manner. The wish not to cause embarrassment is so deep-seated that in business negotiations a Thai will often get a middle man to act for him, thus averting the risk of a direct confrontation.

Such old-world courtesies derive from the rigidly stratified society of the past—not that there has ever been a Thai "class structure" of the sort familiar in European social history. Except among a small, privileged group of people who bear royal titles, social status in Thailand has always been determined primarily by non-hereditary factors, including age, education and—most significant of all—occupation. Until its reform in the late 19th Century, an elaborate system called *sakdi na* (meaning "power over fields") was the main determinant of the social status, landholding and wealth of every freeman in the kingdom, from senior minister down to lowliest peasant. In the upper ranks of the hierarchy were administrative officials selected by the king to serve in the capital or the provinces. Such officials were granted a generous acreage of irrigated rice-field (perhaps as much as 4,000 acres for senior ministers ranging down to about 1,000 acres for junior appointees), and the bulk of their incomes came from the crops. High *sakdi na* rank qualified the holders to be "patrons" with rights to a certain amount of free labour every year from "clients"—low-ranking freemen who, in addition to tilling their own smallholdings (usually no more than about 10 acres of rice-land), did unpaid work for various of the king's appointees. To gain exemption from this forced labour, many clients chose to sell out and become the "slaves" of a chosen patron. This form of slavery, never so harsh as the system common in the Americas, guaranteed food and security both for the man who had sold himself and his whole family, and by the mid-19th Century about a quarter of the Thai population were slaves of this sort. The institution was finally abolished in 1905 as part of the modernizing process of King Chulalongkorn.

Beneath the most junior royal appointee was a whole bureaucracy of civil servants, themselves appointed by the administrative officials and having their own perquisites. All these enjoyed almost complete security; they were hardly ever dismissed except in cases of blatant dishonesty or corruption, and they shared in the prestige conferred by *sakdi na*. The advantages of the system were largely responsible for the traditional reluctance of the Thai élite to enter the tough world of commerce.

A street-vendor and her young daughter, perched on wooden stools, serve customers from behind their mobile sweet-stall. The city's hundreds of street-traders are discouraged by fines or eviction from stationing themselves along the crowded main thoroughfares. But wherever they trade, a flourishing business is assured: Thais are addicted to snacks.

Princess Chumbhot of the Thai royal family (left) pauses beside an antique reading-table in her art-filled Suan Pakkad Palace, situated in north-east Bangkok and open to the public. Among its most exquisite attractions is the Lacquer Pavilion (right), a 17th-Century structure that was removed from near the old Thai capital of Ayutthaya and reassembled on its stilts in her gardens. Its name derives from lacquer scenes illustrating the life of the Buddha that decorate an interior wall.

Although the *sakdi na* system has long been extinct, the concept of the kingdom as a society graded chiefly by occupation has been slow to disappear, and even now, when the pursuit of wealth no longer brings social stigma and Thai society is very much more fluid, the ancient sense of hierarchy still prevails. All social relationships tend to be seen as meetings between superiors and subordinates, and a Thai will not be at his ease until he has classified a newcomer into one or other of the two categories. He will still apply the traditional yardsticks of occupation, age and education, though wealth nowadays counts as an additional one.

As one would expect, this sense of hierarchy is most in evidence when royalty are present. Once I happened to arrive a few minutes late at a tea-party given at Chulalongkorn University in honour of the King's sister. The only chair still vacant at the long table was one next to Her Royal Highness. Being a newcomer at the time and still ignorant of the strictness of Thai protocol, I sat down beside her and was so charmingly welcomed that I soon felt entirely at ease—until I heard the Dean mutter "That won't do at all", and was ignominiously ordered to remove myself.

Hierarchy also lies at the very core of family life, and if a visitor wishes to seek out the roots of Thai formality, it is to the family that he should look, particularly an extended or "joint" family grouping of several branches and generations. Many families of reasonable means live en masse, in a compound of houses and cottages. The poor, who cannot arrange their accommodation so grandiosely, tend to be more fragmented; but even a working-class family group may sometimes occupy a big house together.

In this miniature society, bound together by ties of blood, respect for seniority is obligatory—just as obligatory as the respect that was traditionally

owed to the divinely appointed king, whose "family" was the entire nation. There is no place for permissive innovations, no self-conscious attempt to promote a breezy camaraderie between the generations. The Thai vocabulary of kinship emphasizes the age disparity between the speaker and the person spoken to. Either one is older, and therefore in a position of authority, or else younger and obliged politely to submit.

Duties to a host of relatives are vitally important. Especially among the middle and upper levels of society, social calls paid on innumerable aunts, uncles and cousins take up a large slice of everyone's leisure time. Attending obsequies, the birthdays of elders, weddings and house-warming parties involving religious rites are also virtually imperative. Fortunately these functions are more often enjoyable than not, for the Thais feel happy in a crowd and like to offer hospitality on a generous scale.

Obsequies for the dead are especially elaborate. Instead of the traditional Asian mourning colour—white—women in Bangkok nowadays wear black; men wear white suits with black tie and armband. The rites, usually held in a special building provided in the temple courtyard of a wat, start with the mourners paying their respects and asking for forgiveness by pouring a few drops of lustral water on the hands of the corpse, which has been laid out in readiness. The body is then placed in a coffin and for seven evenings or more—the wealthier or more eminent the deceased, the longer the period—mourners sit before the coffin while monks intermittently chant the Buddhist scriptures. Finally, while relatives and friends pile sticks of incense on a token fire, the body itself is cremated in an electric furnace concealed in a *chedi*-like structure in the monastery courtyard.

However harrowing these protracted rites may be, the bereaved do not allow their grief to discomfort the friends who gather about them at such times. Buddhists are taught to accept death with a calmness appropriate to the inevitable; and a too open display of sorrow is thought slightly improper. Indeed, if the dead person had a successful life, full of merit-making activities, the mood of the mourners may be only relatively subdued.

Unlike funerals, weddings have no great religious significance or scriptural sanction; they are always held in a house or hired hall. Legally, marriage only requires registration with the authorities. Nevertheless, various Brahmanic ceremonials—that is, rites of Hindu origin—have been retained by the people; usually several monks are invited to chant auspicious *sutras* (scriptural texts) a few hours before the ceremony and to receive offerings of food, everyday necessities, and donations of money for their monastery. These gifts are bestowed by relatives on behalf of the bridal couple, and are thought to promote their chance of happiness. (There are lucky months and days for marriages, too, and astrologers are often consulted before the wedding-day is decided on.)

The first wedding I attended in Bangkok was typical of middle- and upper-class ceremonies. At one end of the hired hall, bride and bride-

A passing garbage collector stares vacantly at an advertisement promising armed security protection to purchasers of expensive Western-style homes.

groom, dressed in spotless white, knelt side by side, their forearms supported by cushions on a low table in such a way that their hands, extended as though in prayer, projected over a gilded basin. An old man, respected by both families, dipped his finger in a fragrant paste and traced auspicious marks on the couple's foreheads. Then the guests took turns pouring lustral water from a sacred conch shell on to the couple's hands, while murmuring a few words of advice or good wishes. Being a Thai ceremony it was performed gracefully, but in a manner not too solemn. A witty remark would win from bride or groom an appreciative smile or a soft laugh in reply. By this simple rite the couple were married and a feast for some two hundred people followed.

Once marriages were almost always arranged. Nowadays love-matches are common, but it often happens that parents or other relatives have had a large share in bringing them about. The young women have a Jane Austen-like tendency to avoid bestowing their hearts upon youths unacceptable to their elders. Courtship, too, is still bound by restrictions: though Thais are second to none in their amiability, public displays of affection are held in check by unwritten rules that, to a Westerner, seem positively Victorian. Though you might well see two Thai men holding hands as they walk along a Bangkok pavement—a gesture of ordinary friendship and nothing more—the sight of a man and a woman doing so is rare. During the Vietnam War, American servicemen on leave in Bangkok were inclined to break these behavioural taboos when they went out with bar girls; as a result, some well-brought-up Thai girls were reluctant even to be seen in the company of foreign men.

Young Thais who study in the West sometimes return to Bangkok with foreign wives in tow, but life for these women is likely to be difficult and sometimes unhappy, no matter how hard their husbands strive to please. Once, while working for a United Nations organization in Bangkok, I had as my secretary a vivacious English girl, married to a Thai. "I've had as much of Thailand as I can take," she confided one day, "so I've persuaded my husband to go back to England with me and try to get a job there."

"Jenny, I thought you *liked* Bangkok."

"So I do. Who wouldn't? Everyone's been so kind. But my husband comes from a wealthy family, so he's expected to live in the family compound. Oh, we've a lovely bungalow to ourselves—very private, you'd think—but the servants gossip and his mother knows every little thing I do. If my husband's dining out, I can't even go alone to a 7 o'clock cinema without getting into trouble.

"His mother doesn't exactly scold me, but she hints that married women should be careful of their reputation. When I told my husband that I felt like a prisoner, he said it would be easier for us to go and live in England, since his mother would be dreadfully hurt if we moved out of the compound to set up house anywhere else in Bangkok."

Leaving a memorial service held at Wat Po a hundred days after the death of a respected businessman, a mourner passes an impressive array of floral tributes. The bodies of wealthy people may be preserved at a wat for a year or more before cremation, allowing family members and friends to attend numerous mourning rites and thus earn maximum merit.

I sympathized with Jenny but I also admired her husband's generosity in exiling himself rather than insist she submit to the rigours of the joint family system. Thais, of course, do not see them as rigours. Indeed, their family feeling is so strong that they seem eager to extend the bonds of kinship as far as they will stretch; they address almost everyone they know as Uncle, Aunt, Brother or Sister. In the lane where I live, most people call me Daddy, whether or not they happen to know my name.

If foreign wives find Bangkok's marital customs onerous, the reason almost invariably is the dominance of elders over the young, not inequality between the sexes. Although a well-bred Thai wife might allow herself to appear slightly subordinate to her husband, the reality is often very different. By Asian standards, Thai women have always had a remarkable degree of financial independence. Up to the last century, when Thai men thought commerce beneath their dignity, buying and selling was left largely to foreigners and women. Today a surprising number of Bangkok's business magnates are women. What is more, Thai parents tend to leave house property to their daughters as a safeguard against broken marriage (a house-owning wife with rent coming in can leave an over-bearing husband without fear of penury). In many Bangkok families the women rule the roost, taking over their husbands' pay packets and controlling the domestic economy. This practice may well account for the widespread feeling that, to obtain favours from an official, the surest way is to make oneself useful to his wife.

More than one writer has affirmed that, in the East Asian countries generally, women possess more initiative and other sterling qualities than men. I personally can report that in Bangkok's universities one does get the impression that the female students are more determined to get to the top than the men. The reason may be that the upper- and middle-class Thai girls of today are made more ambitious by the recollection that, a century ago, education was strictly a male preserve. Or it may simply be that life in Bangkok provides fewer distractions for girls than for men.

One thing is certain: the women of Bangkok are too wise to exploit their gains in the war between the sexes very openly. The most ardent feminists display all the womanly charm and graces that Thai men might expect of them, even when they are fighting to remove the last traces of inequality between the sexes. The most striking inequality is the stricter standard applied to women in the matter of adultery. Wives are supposed to be faithful—but not necessarily husbands. Although a man may divorce his wife on grounds of adultery, a woman who divorces her husband for the same reason incurs social stigma. This discrepancy is a leftover from the days when polygamy was still common among the élite of Thailand. The practice did not end until 1935, when an act was passed refusing legal status to a second wife; in addition, if today a man wants children of such a relationship to be included among his legitimate heirs, he must formally recognize them.

Nevertheless, custom still expects that women view their husbands' infidelities lightly; and generally they appear to do so, provided that their husbands do not allow private pleasures to undermine their sense of family responsibility or detract from their wives' dignity. Once, when I dropped round to visit a lawyer friend of mine, I was received by his wife, a still beautiful woman in her early forties. "You should know better than to look for my husband at home on a Friday or Saturday evening," she said, "but whether he amuses himself with only one little 'clientess' or enough to run a beauty contest, I really do not know."

"Well, well," I replied, having acquired the Thai habit of smoothing troubled waters, "I imagine distinguished lawyers have many calls on their time. I dare say his clients are quite elderly and boring."

"Don't bother to excuse him," she replied, "It doesn't upset me in the least. Now that polygamy is illegal and quite out of fashion, it's not to be expected that husbands spend all their spare time at home. My husband is a good man, as men go. He dotes on the children and—*when* at home—behaves well to me. He even allows me the final word in the disposal of our income. So truly things are better as they are.

"My grandmother was one of four wives. There was a house for each of them, of course, and my grandfather dutifully spent a lot of time with his senior—that is, his first—wife, as well as with the youngest, whom he adored. But the two in the middle—my grandmother was one—seldom saw him at all. That sort of thing is long past, I'm glad to say. Do let me give you a glass of whisky and soda, and let's talk of something more amusing."

Midday Dreamers

Few cities are less conducive to midday labour than Bangkok, which endures high humidity from March to September and energy-sapping noontime heat practically all year round. For many citizens, a post-lunch nap is irresistible.

Office workers may return to their homes for a doze, but humbler folk are content with any patch of shade they can find. A sampling of sleepers is pictured here. A bus-driver stretches out in curtained comfort in the aisle of his bus (top row, right), leaving his sandals outside, as tradition dictates. A klong boatman lets his transistor radio play unheeded as he drifts into unconsciousness (top row, left). A weary delivery boy snatches a few minutes of slumber in the back of a truck (middle row, left), while a porter (bottom row, right) simply tips his convey-ance to form a bed with a wicker canopy. And if nothing better is available, a concrete slab on a building site (centre) or the cement floor of a bus-stop (bottom row, left) provide comfort enough when sleep calls.

In Thai eyes, this attitude on the wife's part is an example of good breeding. Why meet difficulties head on when, with a little patience, they may subside of themselves? Such forbearance ensures that divorce in Thailand is relatively uncommon. But just occasionally, when the natural hot-bloodedness that lies beneath the Thai people's serene exterior breaks out, women have been known to kill an unfaithful husband, or so to mutilate him as to make unfaithfulness impossible.

Among the poor—partly because informal unions are regarded as an acceptable form of marriage, partly because couples are unable to afford the expense of a wedding feast for hordes of relatives—people tend simply to live together; and the man, bound by no legal tie, often goes off with another woman. Even then, it is remarkable how often a wife deserted in this way will accept her lot with apparent cheerfulness and set about the task of rearing the children unaided.

Such equanimity is no more, I would argue, than the obverse face of Thai conformity. Rooted deep in the past and in the family, conformity gives stability and promotes a way of life in Bangkok that I believe to be generally a happy one. But a woman colleague of mine at Chulalongkorn University feels I am being over-generous in my estimation of the character of the modern Bangkok Thais.

"It's true that we're an easy-going and tolerant people," she said, "but doesn't that blunt the intellect rather? How many Thais are great readers—1 per cent? And we haven't produced a single scholar or scientist of international repute. Why do you suppose faculty members are required to sign in and out, morning and afternoon, like workmen? It's because we may be too easy-going to do our work conscientiously."

It is probably true that the Thais are natural artists rather than intellectuals. Even among the many urbane, witty people in Bangkok who are able to discourse well on learned subjects, serious attention to philosophy is rare. When life is sweet, as it usually is for the wealthy intelligentsia, there is a reluctance to ponder its meaning.

"Thanks to Buddhism," my colleague continued, "we do have a kind of tranquil cheerfulness, I suppose. But we also suffer from a terrible impetuosity. I daren't think how we would have developed if we had not been Buddhists. Similarly, our respect for elders may be attractive, but I think it breeds a subservience to authority that is—well, not pretty. Our conformity is positively stifling. Can you really approve of our attitude towards even mild eccentricity?"

I confessed I could not. I remember that an Indian pundit was once engaged by the university to teach Sanskrit. His remarkable scholarship cut little ice with his students or other members of the faculty, simply because it struck them as being utterly outlandish that he should wear his hair in a bun, as some Indian scholars do.

Two youngsters hoist the Thai flag at morning assembly outside a primary school at Wat Prang Luang. The education of children rested largely in the hands of Buddhist monks until the turn of the century, and many primary schools are still to be found in the grounds of temples— although the teachers are now government-trained and the curriculum is secular.

Indeed, Thai conformity is most obvious in precisely those places where in the West it is supposedly most absent: the institutions of higher education. All were founded in this century, and they owe much to European and American models. Yet, with the partial exception of the engineering schools and technical colleges, they are run according to old and familiar Thai traditions. Reverence for teachers remains strong: for example, girl students sometimes kneel beside a teacher's desk when they come to ask questions; and during a ceremony held once a year, the student body assembles to offer flowers and incense to the teachers and to ask formally for their blessing. Schoolteachers are addressed as *khru*, which literally means guru; university lecturers are called *acharn*, from the Sanskrit word *acharya*, meaning a person learned in spiritual matters.

Such is the regard for decorum and for teachers that I find it hard to know what students are really thinking. An extreme form of diffidence known as *gring chai*—an awed respect for one's superiors that is intimately bound up with the hierarchical structure of Thai society—makes them hesitant to ask questions or, in speaking or writing, to express views likely to differ from those of a teacher. Were I to state something patently untrue, my students would probably accept it without a murmur, giving no clue whether they did so out of politeness, or because they could not bring themselves to believe that a supposedly wise *acharn* could be wrong. Many years ago, in my eagerness to make a class reveal their own thinking, I went so far as to promise higher marks for papers containing individual expressions of opinion.

"Please do not, Acharn," they protested. "Why should those of us who, in fact, agree with you lose marks for saying what we really think?"

Such deference does indeed have its drawbacks, but at least it helps to promote social stability—a rare blessing in modern South-East Asia. In the eyes of the Thai authorities, docile students are likely to become docile adults, well suited to Bangkok's pyramidal society. Certainly among the middle and upper classes the respect for seniority is still deeply instilled into the young, and it is reinforced by the Buddhist notion that people in high positions deserve reverence, because they owe their good fortune to merits accumulated in former lives.

But by no means all students in higher education conform to traditional standards nowadays. Especially at Thammasat University, which has a strong bias towards the social sciences, surreptitious Marxists and others have been questioning the old forms, and they were among the organizers of the big student demonstrations in 1973 and 1976. At the engineering and technical colleges, which do not have university status and offer mainly vocational courses, the students are even less tractable.

Technical subjects are often still regarded as an educational second-best in Thailand. The brightest and best-qualified students, whose parents have been able to send them to good schools, still aspire to a degree at one of the universities, and many go on to high posts in the civil service. Students at the technical colleges, on the other hand, generally lack the qualifications for university entrance and often come from underprivileged backgrounds. Given the still undeveloped state of the Thai economy and the lack of good openings in industry, they will have lower-than-average job opportunities when they leave. They tend to view decorous behaviour as a luxury in which only the well-to-do can afford to indulge. They also bitterly envy the opportunity at the universities to study side by side with girls, of whom there are very few in the technical colleges. In the troubled years between 1973 and 1976, they were frequently on the rampage, attacking university students with bottle-bombs or fighting among themselves. At times armed warfare between rival engineering schools was a weekly, if not daily, occurrence. Tradition's grasp on the technical college students had become weak, and the only hold on their Thai hot-bloodedness was fear of the consequences of continued violence.

At the time of these upheavals, the peace of Chulalongkorn's campus, with its nucleus of temple-like buildings, green lawns, shady trees and lotus ponds, was for short periods shattered by the strident voices of student orators equipped with amplifiers, and by the shouts of youngsters marching in procession. But generally, when law and order is maintained by military rulers, and cautious optimism is the prevailing mood in politics, traditional Thai-Buddhist virtues come to the fore. The peace of the university campus is disturbed only by the sound of animated conversation and the laughter of groups of young people sitting with their books and the inevitable snacks—for which Thais have a weakness at all times of the day—laid out on tables beneath the trees. Sunlight glistens on the orange-tiled roofs. Well-fed campus dogs lounge about the lawns, too lazy to importune the students, but deigning to accept remnants of food thrown to them. The many-headed *nagas* guarding the flights of stone steps leading up to the class-room verandahs survey all comers in motionless contentment. From a gable of the Arts Building the image of Sarasvati, goddess of the arts, gazes down benignly, impartially bestowing her gifts upon everyone who comes to spend four years beneath her sway.

At the head of the great staircase in the Arts Building, there hangs a portrait of King Chulalongkorn, in whose honour the university was founded in 1917, with an altar-like table in front of it. When examinations or important sports contests are looming, many students offer lighted incense there and pray to his spirit for success. Most students, as they mount the stairs on their way to class, place their palms together in respectful greeting. Seeing them, a visitor might well assume that nothing here had changed since the days of absolute monarchy.

I think of this cheerful tranquillity and conformity as the essence of Thai-ness. How long it can survive in the face of Western materialism and Eastern Communism is hard to say. Already many Thais have been disorientated by the West, whose technical and even political achievements are much admired. Yet there is a feeling, too, that the direct, get-things-done Western approach is insensitive and unsubtle. And to many, Communism seems a bleak and alien alternative.

"In our hearts," confided a Thai friend of mine, "we feel sure that our ways are best."

In Search of Good Fortune

Anxious about examination grades and future prospects, two Bangkok schoolgirls listen intently as a fortune-teller reads cards for them in Lumpini Park.

Ever since the 13th Century, the Thais have been Buddhists—yet the concentration of Buddhism on ultimately transcending the cares of this world has left room for a wealth of beliefs that address concerns in the here and now. When facing an important business transaction, embarking on a journey, grappling with illness or perhaps simply waiting for a winning lottery ticket to be chosen, the people of Bangkok often look to Hindu customs and to folk beliefs that flourished before Buddhism arrived. Supernatural favour and guidance may be sought privately by leaving gifts at shrines where spirits are thought to reside. It is also offered by such specialists as fortune-tellers, astrologers and faith-healers. Buddhism tolerates such practices among the laity—and supernatural aid is often provided by Buddhist monks themselves.

A smartly dressed palmist uses a magnifying glass to follow the palm lines of a young client. His box of equipment includes a picture of the nine kings of the Chakri dynasty, who hold semi-divine status among the Thais and thereby confer authority on his predictions.

While her friend looks on, a woman releases nine eels into the lily-strewn waters of a klong— a ritual intended to reverse a spell of domestic troubles. Nine is considered a lucky number in Thailand, and the setting free of long water creatures, such as eels, is thought to bring a person a long period of good fortune.

Surrounded by enormous phalluses symbolizing the Hindu god Shiva, a woman holds sticks of burning incense as she prays for children at the fertility shrine of S

ao Mae Tap Tim, set in a privately owned garden in east Bangkok. Thailand's cult of phallus worship originated in neighbouring Cambodia some seven centuries ago.

Hanging from a banyan tree at Wat Po, south of the Grand Palace, a series of X-rays chart the condition of a man who is suffering from pulmonary tuberculosis. Wat Po is a centre for faith-healing, and the X-rays will assist monks in deciding whether the case can be helped by a folk cure—anything from the drawing of magical diagrams, perhaps, to pills made from ground-up sacred writings. The banyan tree itself has supernatural significance: according to an ancient Hindu belief, the god Brahma was himself transformed into a banyan.

A crippled patient—one of many who come to Wat Po each day for treatment—makes the "wai" gesture as a faith-healing monk pours holy water over him.

During ceremonies to inaugurate a new bank in Bangkok, customers busy themselves opening accounts while monks—including the Supreme Patriarch (first fr

it) —recite auspicious chants on a platform festooned with gifts. Chapters of Buddhist monks are often invited to confer their blessings on commercial establishments.

3
The Lords of Life

A few years ago I was invited to attend a royal garden party in Bangkok. The World Fellowship of Buddhists was holding a conference in the city, and His Majesty King Bhumibol Adulyadej had asked the participants to meet him—not in the modern Chitralada Palace where he now resides, but in the more romantic Grand Palace. In accordance with protocol, the guests stood in line for presentation to the King, who walked from one end of the line to the other shaking hands with the foreigners, including myself, and receiving low bows or curtseys from the Thais, since custom precludes any physical contact between the King and his own subjects.

Standing next to me was a senior Thai dignitary who, when the King had passed by, suddenly seized my right hand and stroked it with a curious scraping motion. "Do excuse me," he said wistfully, "but I can't help envying you. Though I have served His Majesty for many years, I have never enjoyed the privilege you had just now of actually clasping his hand. The royal touch confers immense good fortune, so perhaps you'll permit me to secure a modest share of the merit bestowed on you." That the King should have power to confer so great a blessing may seem rather surprising, but he is held in unique reverence, not only in court circles but throughout most of Thailand.

Although the monarchy was shorn of its absolute powers half a century ago, Thais continue to look upon their King as near-divine, a being whose ability to intercede with the gods is considered essential to national survival and prosperity. When he leaves his palace to visit any other part of the city, police officers wearing ceremonial swords, but also equipped with walkie-talkies and other modern gear, line the route and hold up traffic for several minutes as the procession of cars containing the royal entourage approaches. But this inconvenience is not in the least resented by motorists, since even a momentary glimpse of the King as his car flashes by is deemed to avert bad luck for seven years. My youngest daughter, a Thai teenager whom I adopted when she was two, will gladly walk a mile or more and stand in the hot sun for an hour if a rumour reaches her that the King is expected to drive by. And elderly people are just as eager to make merit in this way.

Judging from the little that is known of early Thai history, the monarchs originally had none of these godlike attributes. In the 13th Century, the kings of Sukhothai were content to be treated simply as *Pho Meung*—Fathers of the Country—and were prepared to meet their people without pomp and ceremony. Ramkhamhaeng, who reigned from the late 1270s

At a religious ceremony held in the Temple of the Emerald Buddha, a woman crouches to receive the blessing of King Bhumibol. The custom requiring all subjects to make obeisance in this way was relaxed by the King's grandfather in 1873, but many Thais still regard their monarchs with a reverence akin to worship.

to the end of the 13th Century and was the inventor of the Thai script, encouraged his subjects to approach him informally, whether to make a petition or for any other reason. A stone pillar near the palace entrance bore an inscription urging anyone troubled by controversies "or matters that distress them within and cramp their hearts" to ring a bell and summon the King to offer judgment.

The later concept of godlike kingship came, like many other Thai beliefs, from Cambodia. Ever since the founding of the kingdom of Sukhothai in 1238, the Thais had been politically independent of their former Khmer overlords, but after the eclipse of Sukhothai by the rival Thai kingdom of Ayutthaya in the late 14th Century, they fell more and more under the cultural influence of Cambodia. The Cambodian rulers were attended by Brahman priests and worshipped as god-kings. The Thais, though retaining their Buddhist faith, soon invested their own kings with similar attributes; they also adopted the elaborate ceremonies surrounding a Hindu ruler, a special vocabulary to be used in addressing him, and some very high-sounding royal epithets. Chief among them was *Chao Chiwit*, or Lord of Life. It was not an exaggerated term of respect for these absolute monarchs. They owned all the land and resources of the kingdom and could grant a man wealth and status or, on the instant, order him to be executed. Although the king retained his patriarchal role as Father of the Country, he was henceforth more often treated with a degree of reverence that amounted to worship. To this day, the phrase used for "I" when speaking to the monarch is *"Kha Phra Buddha Chao"*, meaning "I, the slave of the Lord Buddha", which seems to imply that the king is in some way identified with the Buddha.

During the four centuries that Ayutthaya was the Thai capital (from 1350 to 1767), the monarchy reached a pinnacle of power and splendour. The king was seen as mediator between the people and the gods, harmonizing the human world with the cosmic order. The royal palace was identified with Phra Meru, the sacred mountain that in Hindu belief stood at the centre of the universe. All those who shared the king's roof were regarded as co-residents of the celestial heights, thereby sharing the monarch's sanctity. Lower officials or servants were required to prostrate themselves in the presence of such persons and the penalty for touching any member of the royal entourage was decapitation.

The royal palace was the seat of government and each high official was courtier, soldier and civil servant rolled into one. Most senior appointments went to the king's close relatives—exceedingly numerous, since a monarch might well have 50 or 60 consorts. Polygamy on so grand a scale served to bind powerful noblemen to the throne by ties of consanguinity, and the habit of appointing royal offspring to the most important positions in the state also helped to satisfy high-born and possibly dangerous ambitions.

Sons of the king shared his divinity in varying degrees, according to the

Holding lotus flowers she hopes to present to the King when he emerges from the Temple of the Emerald Buddha, a woman humbly squats beside an armed guard. Traditionally given to monks and royalty, the lotus symbolizes Enlightenment because it rises from mud, just as Buddhism rises above earthly corruption.

status of their mothers. As many as three or four royal consorts might simultaneously enjoy the rank of queen, and any son or daughter of theirs was known as *Chao Fa*, or Celestial Prince and Princess. Children of other royal wives were a rung lower in status; from the end of the 18th Century on, they were styled *Phra Ong Chao*—literally "Royal Body" Prince or Princess. If these titles had been handed down from generation to generation in perpetuity, they would have multiplied so many times as to become banal. Accordingly, a system was devised so that the grand-children and great-grandchildren of the king received titles in descending order of importance, and the children of the fifth, or in some cases the sixth generation (depending on the rank of their original royal ancestor), reverted to the status of commoner.

Since the accession of King Prajadhipok in 1925, the Thai kings have been strict monogamists, and nowadays celestial princes and princesses (addressed as Your Royal Highness) are comparatively rare. But a sub-stantial number of people in Bangkok still bear the less exalted royal titles of *Mom Chao* (usually translated as Serene Highness, the last rank to carry the style Prince or Princess in English), *Mom Rachawong* (applied to children of a *Mom Chao*) and *Mom Luang* (applicable to grandchildren). Many *moms* possess considerable landed wealth—though nothing to match the large estates inherited by the King—and a handful receive the annual government subsidies paid to major royal personages. There are *moms* nowadays who acquit themselves well as scholars, diplomats, patrons of the arts and public figures; but others, disgusted by the poor performance of governments since 1932, have preferred voluntary retirement from public life.

One of them, the late Prince Subhasvasti, took an active part in the Free Thai Movement during his country's occupation by the Japanese in the Second World War. After the war, he withdrew to a country estate and took up fruit-growing. His nostalgia for the old regime caused him to continue flying the old Siamese flag with its proud white elephant; and once, when I visited him at his residence, he greeted me with the words: "Well, John, how nice that you have got away from Thailand and come to stay in Siam for a while!" A few *moms* have fallen upon bad times, among them a lady *Mom Luang* who actually answered my advertisement for a cook. Thinking she would be likely to know some recondite Thai dishes, I went to fetch her to my house to discuss matters with my wife; but on the way, she chided me so royally for my bad driving that I thought it better to choose a cook from a more humble walk of life.

Throughout the era of absolute monarchy, the hereditary principle, even in the form of constantly diminishing importance, was absent from the rest of Thai society. There was no hereditary aristocracy: nobles were appointed by the king and did not pass on their titles at death. The monarchy itself remained non-hereditary until the principle of primo-

Garnished with red flower petals, seed rice grown in the King's own paddy-fields awaits the ritual sowing.

A Royal Rice Ritual

By far the most important crop grown in Thailand is rice; and traditionally rice-farmers look to the King, as divine guardian of the land, to assure their prosperity. Every May, he inaugurates the planting season by sponsoring the Ploughing Ceremony, a ritual rooted in ancient Brahmanic beliefs and staged at the Pramane Ground, near the Grand Palace. The King's role as ploughman is delegated to an Agriculture Ministry official —known for that day as the Harvest Lord— who guides the ox-drawn implement and then scatters seed rice. Afterwards, Brahman priests offer the oxen a selection of food and drink, and predict the harvest prospects on the basis of what the animals choose.

Crowds at the Pramane Ground gaze at the sacred plough, held in a special mount, before the ceremony begins.

As an ox chooses from a platter of seven varieties of food, a white-garbed Brahman ponders the harvest omens.

Identified by his conical white hat, the Harvest Lord walks behind the plough, while Brahmans in the vanguard sprinkle holy water and blow on conch shells.

Four "Celestial Maidens"—roles played by government officials—carry gold and silver baskets of rice that will be sown in the new furrows by the Harvest Lord.

geniture was introduced as the sole qualification for accession in 1895. In earliest times there had been no rules for deciding the succession to the throne. To reduce the consequent rivalry and dissension within the royal family, King Trailok in 15th-Century Ayutthaya started the practice of designating an heir apparent. The king's choice had to be confirmed by an electoral council of princes, prelates and nobles. Generally the council followed a king's wishes—but only if its members were convinced that the candidate was well qualified to exercise the high powers that would be vested in him as the Lord of Life.

Having ascended the Ayutthayan throne, the kings were responsible to no one—not even, like medieval sovereigns in Europe, to God. But they were expected to conduct themselves according to 10 rules of kingly behaviour that originated in India: charity, morality, rectitude, justice, compassion, restraint, energy, mercy, forbearance and conciliation. The kings presided over numerous religious rites, including the annual Ploughing Ceremony—a ritual rice-sowing designed to ensure a bountiful harvest— and the offering of raiment and other necessities to chapters of monks. To reinforce their sanctity and power in the eyes of the people, they undertook lavish temple-building projects. Like Europe's medieval rulers, they frequently journeyed through their kingdom to display their might and wealth, sometimes travelling along the network of canals and rivers in royal barges ornamented with figure-heads of mythical beasts and demons, sometimes riding on elephant back.

Most curious of the Thai kings' up-country engagements were the periodic hunts for so-called white elephants—creatures considered so auspicious that every ruler longed to possess a large number of them. Although they are albinos, these elephants are in fact far from white and can be identified only by some light-coloured areas around the eyes, ears and feet. Their presence in the royal stable was believed to ensure prosperity for the entire realm.

From the moment of their capture in the jungle, such elephants were treated with immense respect. They were accorded high-sounding official titles, formal enrolment in the civil service and rich stipends to pay for housing, fodder, ceremonial trappings and retinues of attendants who provided for their every need. Their food was sometimes served on trays of gold and silver. Special musicians and singers were appointed to entertain them, and on ceremonial occasions they might be decked out with up to 200 pounds of gold ornaments. The high officials charged with looking after the elephants and their entourages often found the task extremely burdensome—hence the phrase "a white elephant", meaning a troublesome possession. Nowadays, white elephants, when identified, are invariably presented to the King and kept at the Chitralada Palace, though they are no longer splendidly adorned.

During Ayutthayan times the white elephants were so highly regarded

A Succession of Kingdoms

9th-12th Century A.D.	Thai peoples begin to migrate from south-west China into the region comprising modern Burma, Laos and Thailand. The Thais who settle along the upper tributaries of the Chao Phya River in north Thailand encounter the Khmer (Cambodian) empire
1238	Thai chieftain, Sri Intaratitya, defeats Khmer rulers in the north and sets up an independent Thai state centred on the conquered city of Sukhothai
1253	Kublai Khan and his Mongol armies invade south-west China, giving further impetus to the southerly movement of the Thais into the new kingdom of Sukhothai and other Thai principalities
1279-1298	Reign of King Ramkhamhaeng the Great, marking the start of an absolute monarchy. The King creates the first Thai alphabet, based on Khmer script, and fosters the arts. Buddhism is made the official religion
1350	City of Ayutthaya founded on an island in Chao Phya River, 55 miles north of present-day Bangkok, as capital of a newly emergent southern Thai state
1389	Thais attack Khmer capital, Angkor Thom, capturing some 90,000 people; Khmer court rituals and law are subsequently adopted by the Thais, with local modifications, and the Hindu-based Khmer notion of the god-king is introduced into Thai system of kingship
1419	After decades of sporadic warfare, the weakened kingdom of Sukhothai accepts the overlordship of Ayutthaya
1511	First European diplomatic mission, sent by the viceroy of Portuguese India, sails into Gulf of Thailand. Bangkok, a fishing village on eastern side of the Chao Phya River, is used as a way station for foreign travellers awaiting permission to proceed to the royal city of Ayutthaya
1545	Population of Ayutthaya reaches approximately 150,000
1569	Burmese capture Ayutthaya and appoint a vassal-king
1584	Thai military hero, Prince Naresuan, defeats Burmese and evicts them from Ayutthaya
1678	Greek adventurer, Constantine Phaulkon, arrives at Ayutthaya and within five years rises from clerk in the Thai treasury to chief adviser to the King
1685	French diplomatic mission from Louis XIV visits Ayutthaya. The capital, now at the peak of its magnificence, has nearly 400 temples and 35 miles of waterways
1688	Factions hostile to foreigners arrest and behead Phaulkon; Thai leaders sever relations with the West, a break that will last some 150 years
1767	Burmese army captures and totally destroys Ayutthaya; within months the Thai general, Taksin, repels Burmese and proclaims himself king. He establishes a new capital at Thonburi, across the river from the hamlet of Bangkok. Wat Arun (Temple of the Dawn) is founded
1772	King Taksin appoints a valiant follower, General Chakri, as Commander-in-Chief of Thai armies
1778	General Chakri captures the Lao capital of Vientiane and removes the legendary Emerald Buddha to Thonburi
1782	After displaying symptoms of megalomania, King Taksin is executed, and General Chakri—later called Rama I—founds the present Chakri dynasty of Thailand. He moves his capital across the Chao Phya River to Bangkok and builds the Grand Palace complex. The eastern border of the city is marked by construction of a wall and Klong Ong Ang, enclosing a 2½-square-mile area of royal palaces, temples, public and military buildings
1785	Wat Phra Keo built to house the Emerald Buddha
1793	Wat Po (Temple of Reclining Buddha) is built
1822	Envoy of Britain's East India Company, Dr. John Crawfurd, makes an unsuccessful attempt to establish trade relations with Thailand
1850	Rama III begins construction of Bangkok's "Golden Mount", a temple-topped artificial hill replicating a shrine in Ayutthaya. It will be completed 28 years later, during the reign of Rama V

that in the 1550s they precipitated the first of the many wars between the Thai kingdom and Burma, whose ruler envied the Thai king's possession of a large stableful. These were the conflicts that led eventually to the destruction of Ayutthaya in 1767.

The task of rebuilding the fortunes of the kingdom and creating a new capital of suitable grandeur fell to the kings of the present Chakri dynasty, inaugurated in 1782 with the crowning of General Chakri at Bangkok. Ruling as absolute monarchs until 1932, and thereafter as constitutional monarchs, Chakri kings presided over their country's entry into the modern world—its opening to international trade and to the ideas and institutions of the West. In a turmoil of rapid changes, they maintained an exceptional social and political stability; two 19th-Century members of the dynasty—Mongkut and Chulalongkorn—were to be reformers of the first order.

At first, however, the aim of the Chakri kings was to lift Thai culture again to the heights attained during the Ayutthayan period. The challenge was a formidable one. Almost the entire corpus of Thai literature—inscribed on pages of palm-leaf, since printing was almost unknown in the kingdom—had been housed in the libraries and palaces of the old capital. The burning of the city was thus not only a political and military disaster, but a literary catastrophe whose full extent will never be known. Under the patronage of the Chakri kings, however, Thai literature flowered again, especially resplendent in highly stylized verse forms. Rama I was himself a poet of some distinction. Under his personal supervision, scholars who had studied in Ayutthaya re-compiled from memory the innumerable stanzas of the Thai epic poem, the *Ramakien*. Based on the ancient Indian *Ramayana*, it recounts the life of the legendary hero, Prince Rama, and has provided many themes of Thai painting, sculpture and classical dance.

Traditional painting, apart from charming decorative patterns of foliage, flowers, birds and insects, consisted largely of murals depicting episodes from legendary tales—in particular the *Ramakien*. Some of the finest and most entertaining examples produced in the new capital were the murals decorating the cloisters of the Temple of the Emerald Buddha. Dating from the second quarter of the last century, the tableaux provide a visual account of the whole *Ramakien* epic and are dominated by the gods, heroes and demons encountered by Prince Rama. These principal figures are depicted with a lavish use of gold paint and brilliant colour. The backgrounds, too, are delightful. They include vistas of walled cities and fabulous palaces; humorous portrayals of domestic, market and river life; and occasionally an amusingly anachronistic 19th-Century steamboat or even a group of Europeans absurdly overdressed for the climate.

Until a century ago, the only education in Bangkok, apart from the mainly religious instruction in the monasteries, was to be had in the palace and in institutions closely connected with it. Young princes and noblemen,

1851 Half-brother of Rama III ascends throne as Rama IV, better known as King Mongkut. Within the next three years, he extends city limits by digging a new enclosing canal, Klong Krung Kasem. Bangkok's population reaches 400,000

1855 King Mongkut signs far-reaching treaty with Sir John Bowring, envoy of Queen Victoria, opening Thailand to British trade and exempting all British subjects in the country from Thai laws. Bangkok's canal system is greatly extended

1862 First major road, Charoen Krung (New Road), is laid out along a former elephant track and becomes one of Bangkok's busiest thoroughfares, lined by foreign trading houses, residences and embassies

1910 Reign of King Chulalongkorn (Rama V), marked by a sweeping modernization of Thai laws and customs. Slavery is abolished. Bangkok becomes one of the largest and most important cities in south-eastern Asia, with a population of 600,000

1899 Wat Benchamabopit, built of Carrara marble, is completed. A reliquary tower is erected on summit of the Golden Mount to house a relic of the Buddha

1910 Chinese, who run most of the commercial enterprises in Bangkok but pay little tax, riot in protest against new poll-tax law. City is paralyzed for four days until the riots are suppressed. Anti-Chinese feelings will linger for decades

1915 National Assembly, designed originally as a throne hall for King Mongkut, is completed

1917 Chulalongkorn University is founded. After the United States enters First World War, Thailand joins Allied Forces

1921 Compulsory elementary education is introduced

1932 Revolutionary group of government officials stage a bloodless coup—the first of 20 that will disrupt Thai political life over the years. King Prajadhipok (Rama VII) consents to become a constitutional monarch

1933 University of Thammasat (originally named the University of Moral and Political Science) founded

1935 King Rama VII, disillusioned with government turmoil, abdicates; his nephew Ananda assumes throne

1939 Official name of country changed from Siam to Thailand—literally, "Land of the Free"

1941 Thailand occupied by Japanese forces; the country is allied to Japan for duration of Second World War

1945 Peace treaties signed between Thailand and Allied Powers

1946 King Ananda is mysteriously killed in his bed; he is succeeded by his younger brother, King Bhumibol (Rama IX)

1949 Immigration quotas reduced to 200 per nation—a move aimed principally at curtailing the influx of Chinese

1954 Thailand becomes a member of SEATO (South-East Asia Treaty Organization)

1960 Population of Bangkok exceeds 1.5 million

1962 United States and Thailand sign a bilateral defence treaty, permitting the establishment of U.S. military bases in Thailand

1963 Military officers Thanom and Prapass succeed to power and establish dictatorial rule for next 10 years

1965 Start of armed insurrection in northern and north-eastern provinces, led by the Communist Party of Thailand. National Theatre (Silpakorn Theatre) is opened

1973 Student demonstrations against military government lead to toppling of regime. Thanom and Prapass leave the country at the King's request and a democratic coalition party government is set up

1976 Following the return of Thanom and Prapass, protesting students and angry right-wing mobs clash at Thammasat University. Forty-six students die and nearly 200 are wounded. Martial law is declared and a military junta takes over.

1978 Population reaches an estimated 4.5 million

In a mural based on tales first recounted in the Hindu epic, the "Ramayana", around 300 B.C., the hero, Prince Rama, relaxes on a curtained bed within the protective jaws of an enormous monkey god. A Thai version of the epic, the "Ramakien", was created under the supervision of King Rama I, who had this mural painted in the Temple of the Emerald Buddha.

besides being trained in etiquette and the martial arts proper to their rank, also became connoisseurs of music and developed literary skills. The high culture of Thailand was kept alive almost entirely by royal patronage.

And yet, to the earliest Europeans who visited Bangkok, the royal court was apt to appear barbaric. One of the first visitors who recorded what he saw was Dr. John Crawfurd, who came to Bangkok in 1822 during the reign of Rama II seeking favourable trading terms for the British East India Company. Describing the Thais as "half-naked and enslaved barbarians", he commented that even ministers and princes were reduced to "beast-like grovelling" in the presence of anyone whose social rank was considered to outstrip their own. He and his party were appalled by the obsequiousness that surrounded the Lord of Life himself. Describing their first royal audience, one of Crawfurd's colleagues wrote: "The whole multitude present lay prostrate on the earth, their mouths almost touching the ground: not a body or limb was observed to move; not any eye was directed towards us; not a whisper agitated the solemn and still air. It was the attitude, the silence, the solemnity of a multitude simultaneously addressing the great God of the universe, rather than the homage of even an enslaved people. Not even Rome, fertile in a race of tyrants, nor Dionysius himself, ever produced any degradation to compare with this in ignominy."

Crawfurd described how, as soon as the audience had ended, "curtains on each side of the throne, moved by some concealed agency, closed upon it. This was followed by the same flourish of wind instruments and the same wild shout which accompanied our entrance; and the courtiers falling upon their faces to the ground, made six successive prostrations."

After three months of futile negotiations, Crawfurd returned to India, empty-handed except for a few purely nominal trade concessions, some sweetmeats and spices, and a set of elephant's teeth. But the empire-building Europeans of those days were not going to be satisfied with this sort of treatment for long. Over the next three decades, the British consolidated their hold on the Malay Peninsula, won two major wars and seized much territory in Burma; and in the Sino-British War of 1839-42 they forced the Manchu Emperor to cede Hong Kong and open five ports to trading vessels of all nations. France was already intervening in the affairs of what was to become French Indo-China. The Thais were faced with the choice either of coming to terms with the Western powers or of being devoured by them.

That the Thais kept their independence was due to the extraordinary foresight and judgment of King Mongkut, who acceded to the throne in 1851 at the relatively advanced age of 47 and reigned for 17 years. It is unfortunate that this outstanding monarch became best known in the West through Anna Leonowens' memoirs. According to Anna, Mongkut "was as fickle and petulant as he was suspicious and cruel". On one occasion, she wrote, the King punished a royal concubine and a monk with whom she

Near the eastern end of Memorial Bridge, a man kneels before a bronze statue of King Rama I, founder of Bangkok, praying for his assistance in some personal matter. The still widespread belief that Thai monarchs possess divine powers was absorbed from Cambodia in the 14th Century.

had committed adultery by having them burned at the stake. Victorian readers must have shuddered at the impression Anna gave of her employer. Equally, they must have thrilled at the portrait she presented of herself as heroine of the royal harem. It was, she wrote, "my consolation to know that I could befriend the women and children of the palace, who, when they saw that I was not afraid to oppose the king in his more outrageous caprices of tyranny, imagined me endued [*sic*] with supernatural powers, and secretly came to me with their grievances, in full assurance that sooner or later I would see them redressed. And so, with no intention on my part, and almost without my own consent, I suffered myself to be set up between the oppressor and the oppressed."

In fact, much of what Anna wrote was simply untrue. Her memoirs were so full of mistakes that no one who reads them now and knows something of the Thais in those days can take them seriously. The hair-raising story of the monk and the concubine was lifted almost word for word from a French account, itself based on hearsay, of an incident falsely rumoured to have taken place in an earlier reign. It is well known that the lady to whom Anna ascribed the dreadful fate of burning at the stake was never arraigned for adultery nor harmed in any way, and actually lived on to become a grandmother. Moreover, when one of Mongkut's consorts did misconduct herself—in this case with a commoner—she suffered no worse punishment than disgrace at court, and her seducer was ordered to pay a very modest fine.

Far from being the tyrant of the harem, Mongkut broke with age-old tradition by granting childless consorts the right to resign at will. As for Anna's claim that she exerted great influence over Mongkut's children, I once met an old gentleman who had been the constant companion of King Chulalongkorn during the last 10 years of that monarch's life. Chulalongkorn in his boyhood had been one of the princes under Anna's charge, and she had claimed credit for building his much admired strength of character. But the old gentleman assured me that he had never once heard the Englishwoman's name pass the royal lips. In a country where teachers are so warmly revered, this evidence is proof of the Englishwoman's total unimportance in the life of Chulalongkorn and his kingdom.

Why should Anna have wished to distort the picture? According to one account, Anna, on leaving the King's service, abruptly demanded £400— perhaps $13,000 today—as a kind of severance pay; when this claim was refused, she tried to get revenge by writing books that would blacken Mongkut's reputation in the eyes of his Western friends, notably Queen Victoria. Anna herself refers to disagreements over pay, though I suspect what caused her most frustration was her failure to become a power behind the throne.

In January 1867, only a few months before Anna set sail for England, the King wrote a revealing note to one of his officials. The English governess, he said, was trying to meddle in his affairs and was becoming "very naughty indeed". Mongkut went on to explain how she had been pestering him to engage the British diplomat, Sir John Bowring, as head of a forthcoming Thai mission to Paris. She had even tried to dictate the salary that Bowring was to be paid. Mongkut concludes his letter with an ironical caricature of himself as fair game for small-minded, mercenary people like Anna: "Oh! The King of Siam has a great pile of money! He is very rich and in possession of absolute power and strange desires, but he is at the same time so cowardly, so stupid and vain as to become an easy prey to money-seekers."

Far from being the barbarian that Anna Leonowens would have us suppose, King Mongkut knew at least 10 ancient and modern languages— including Sanskrit, Pali, English and Latin—and was an accomplished astronomer and historian. From the age of 20, when he was passed over by the electoral council in favour of a half-brother who was less senior by birth but politically more experienced, he had spent his life as a Buddhist monk, learning the arts of meditation, studying with an insatiable curiosity, and meeting Thais of all social strata—a rare advantage for a future king. His search for knowledge also brought him into contact with some of the Christian missionaries who were then starting to enter the country, and, through them, he acquired a unique insight into Western ideas and attitudes. His devotion to Buddhist precepts remained unshaken by these contacts, but by the time he was finally invited to ascend the throne, he had become convinced that the Thais' only hope of political salvation lay through European-style reforms.

Mongkut's programme of changes was far-reaching. He established a Royal Mint in the Grand Palace for the issuance of coinage to replace the lumps of metal and cowrie shells then in use. He discouraged the use of the old forced labour system, preferring instead to hire free labour for public works. With the help of an American missionary friend, he set up a printing-press. He formed a steam-propelled merchant fleet, manned by English captains. He overhauled the legal system, issuing 500 new laws. And he altered his own position by abolishing the old practice of attending court naked to the waist, and by gradually whittling away at the taboos still surrounding the monarchy.

In previous reigns, the common people had been obliged to avert their gaze from the sacred person of the king, under pain of having their eyes shot out by the royal crossbowmen. Because Mongkut wished to be seen by his subjects, he abolished this prohibition and encouraged people to watch royal processions. His predecessor had left the palace only once a year, to visit the temples of Bangkok; but Mongkut soon became a familiar figure, riding on horseback through the countryside or steaming across the Gulf of Thailand aboard the royal paddle-ship. While still a monk, Mongkut had carried out excavations at Sukhothai and had recovered Ramkhamhaeng's

In formal attire, King Mongkut (Rama IV) sits for the 1861 daguerreotype portrait that he sent to Pope Pius IX. Contrary to his posthumous reputation as the benighted sovereign of the musical "The King and I", Mongkut introduced many reforms in Thailand, encouraged the adoption of Western technology and maintained friendly relations with many international leaders.

stone inscription urging aggrieved citizens to ring the bell at the palace gate and present him with their petitions. Mongkut restored this right of royal redress and appeared in person each week to receive his subjects, though petitioners were warned to avoid "subtlety, prevarication and circumlocution", and the use of obscene language was strictly forbidden.

Mongkut's most dramatic break with the past was his policy of collaboration with the West. In 1855, Sir John Bowring arrived in Bangkok as the envoy of Queen Victoria to negotiate a full-scale commercial treaty. Bowring later described how the King received him on a marvellous moonlit night, seated upon an ornamented throne and wearing a crimson dress, a gold girdle and a head-dress glistening with precious jewels. After offering cigars and liqueurs, the King showed Bowring his private apartments. What had impressed the fastidious diplomat about the rest of the Grand Palace were "the barbaric grandeur, the parade, the show, the glitter, the real magnificence", and he was surprised to find how differently Mongkut's inner sanctum was furnished. In addition to a near life-sized statue of Queen Victoria and another of Prince Albert, the royal apartments also contained a great variety of clocks, microscopes, telescopes, barometers, thermometers and other scientific instruments, as well as a large collection of books and handsome writing-desks, "in a word, all the instruments and appliances which might be found in the study or library of an opulent philosopher in Europe".

Unlike Dr. John Crawfurd, his predecessor, Bowring managed in three weeks to obtain practically everything he wanted. The treaty he signed limited the duties on goods imported by British merchants, provided for the appointment of a British consul with complete jurisdiction over all British subjects in the kingdom and regulated the taxes that might be imposed on them. Moreover, Mongkut agreed to lift restrictions on exports. Since rice and teak, the two main Thai products, were then in enormous demand worldwide, this measure gave the Thai economy a great stimulus, as well as enabling traders, many of them Europeans, to make their fortunes. Believing that the best way of keeping Western predators at bay was to give all of them a stake in the kingdom, Mongkut signed similar treaties with France and the United States in 1856, and with other countries in subsequent years.

In his determination to forge links with the West, Mongkut also carried on a prolific correspondence with various heads of state. He initiated an exchange of letters and gifts with Pope Pius IX, and wrote to President Buchanan of the United States offering to send him some transport elephants. An amusing example of Mongkut's diplomatic style was the manner in which he overcame a difficulty that arose in his correspondence with Queen Victoria. He realized there were certain contexts in which she would expect to see the word God mentioned. It was greatly in his interest to stand in good favour with that powerful lady, but as a Buddhist he was

Huge model elephants, symbol of the prestige of Thai monarchs, form a triumphal archway for the return of King Chulalongkorn after a visit to Europe in 1897.

not prepared to use the word. He solved the problem by substituting a phrase of his own invention that would satisfy both of them: "The Super-Agency of the Universe".

In attempting to modernize his country, Mongkut was handicapped by the traditionalism of his subjects, who neither appreciated the importance of Western technology nor recognized the urgent necessity for reform. Before he could accomplish all he wished, he contracted a fatal fever—brought about, ironically, by his passion for astronomy. He had outdone European scientists by calculating the exact moment of the solar eclipse of 1868. Unfortunately, the best vantage point for observing the eclipse was a mosquito-infested region close to the Gulf of Thailand, and there Mongkut caught his fever. Passing away, like the Buddha, on his birthday, he turned—as the Buddha had also done—on to his right side and murmured "This is the correct way to die."

His son Chulalongkorn, who reigned until 1910 as Rama V, energetically continued Mongkut's policies. He abolished slavery and abandoned several ancient royal customs, including ceremonial prostration. His courtiers, to their astonishment, were ordered to stand up in his presence. Chulalongkorn became the first Thai ruler to depart from his kingdom since the campaigns against Burma in the early 17th Century: soon after his accession he travelled to Malaya, Java, Singapore and India. Later he visited Russia, Germany, France and England. What he saw made him even more determined to transform his own country into a modern state.

He brought in foreign advisers to assist in the reorganization of government departments and in the building of railways to link remote provinces with the capital. In turn, many of his 32 sons were sent to Europe to receive the kind of education that would enable them to steer their country towards greater modernization. He warned them against the notion that princes could go through life without doing useful work, and he stressed the purpose of their mission. "If after acquiring proficiency in foreign languages you cannot turn them into Siamese, little advantage will have been gained, for we can employ as many foreigners as we need. What will be required of you is an ability to turn a European language into Siamese, and Siamese into a European language. You would be useful then."

Although Chulalongkorn was surprisingly up to date in many ways, and enthusiastically promoted the Westernization of Bangkok in architecture, road-building, motor transport and administration, he nonetheless clung to some customs of the autocratic past. He was the last Thai monarch to practise polygamy on a grand scale, and under him many old traditions continued to be observed to the letter. Thus, when his favourite queen—whom he loved most tenderly—fell into the Chao Phya River, she was allowed to drown because none of the many onlookers dared lay hands upon her royal person. Chulalongkorn also arranged for each of the newly created government ministries to be run by a celestial prince. The Thais,

A portrait of King Chulalongkorn and the royal family, painted in 1881 by an unknown European artist, dominates a sumptuous chamber in the Grand Palace. During the King's rule from 1868 to 1910, many of Bangkok's major roads, bridges and monuments were built, creating one of the most imposing cities of South-East Asia.

he argued, were not yet ready for anything so drastic as democracy and, until legislators of the right calibre emerged, they were better off under an absolute monarchy.

The practice of giving high administrative posts to men of royal descent became increasingly irksome to the new middle class—the bureaucrats and senior military men who were needed to keep the apparatus of a modern state ticking over. By the early decades of the 20th Century, a number of this new élite had been educated, like their royal masters, in Europe. They finally revolted against a system that excluded even the most brilliant commoner from high office. At dawn on June 24, 1932, soldiers snatched the senior princes from their homes and herded them, still in pyjamas, into the marble throne hall of the Dusit Palace, where they were detained as hostages for several days.

Meanwhile, King Prajadhipok was taking a summer holiday at his seaside palace on the Gulf of Thailand. The day after the detention of the princes, a warship arrived there with an ultimatum from the plotters—a group of civilians and officers who called themselves the Promoters and were acting under the aegis of the newly formed People's Party. In effect, they gave the King two choices. He could either return peacefully to Bangkok and agree to rule as a constitutional monarch, or he could march on the capital with loyal troops from the provincial garrisons and risk the consequences to both his relatives and his country. Being a progressive and cautious monarch, he chose the first course. The princes at the Dusit Palace were released, and on December 10, 1932, King Prajadhipok signed the constitution that brought the ancient power of absolute monarchy to an end.

At the time of the coup, King Prajadhipok had been enthusiastically engaged in preparing a constitution that might have worked more successfully than the nominally democratic system imposed by the coup leaders. He was confused and saddened by the recurrent military dictatorships that followed. Though more often benevolent than harsh, they were far from what the King, or those who supported the original coup, had had in mind. In 1935, King Prajadhipok abdicated while on a visit to England and retired to the small town of Virginia Water outside London, where he died six years later.

He was succeeded by King Ananda, who in 1935 was a 10-year-old boy at school in Switzerland. Ananda did not return permanently to Bangkok until the end of the Second World War. Within months he was found dead in the Grand Palace. His death has never been satisfactorily explained. The present King Bhumibol, Ananda's brother, ascended the throne in 1946, and shortly afterwards married Queen Sirikit, by whom he has four children.

The 20th-Century monarchs of Thailand, if lacking the power of their 19th-Century predecessors, have continued the tradition of cultural

On his coronation day in November 1925, King Prajadhipok (Rama VII) assumes a commanding air while seated on his throne before a retinue of regalia-bearers.

After a processional trip on the Chao Phya River a few months after the coronation, the royal barge brings King Prajadhipok to a landing near the Grand Palace.

accomplishment that is so much a feature of the Chakri dynasty. For example, King Vajiravudh, who succeeded Chulalongkorn as Rama VI in 1910, was a noted poet and playwright, and translated some of Shakespeare's works into Thai. He specialized in skilfully adapting French and English works to make them fit the Thai scene: thus, events originally set in, say, London and the seaside town of Brighton, are cleverly transposed to suit the mode of life in Bangkok and a well-known watering-place on the Gulf of Thailand, Hua Hin.

King Bhumibol—born in Cambridge, Massachusetts, in 1927, while his father, Prince Mahidol, was studying medicine at Harvard University—is very much a man of the present century. He is a keen saxophonist and composer of modern songs, a talented painter, an expert yachtsman and —like his great-grandfather, King Mongkut—an enthusiast in scientific matters. He has thrown himself into all manner of projects: schemes for developing the economy of the northern hill tribes, who have to be weaned from growing opium poppies without losing their tribal identities; the introduction of dairy farming in a country unused to consuming milk products; the establishment of model agricultural co-operatives; and experiments in new farming techniques. He has transformed his Chitralada Palace grounds, once uniformly pastoral, into what looks increasingly like an experimental farm.

Not surprisingly, the royal ceremonial surrounding the King is but a shadow of what it was a century ago. King Bhumibol's ancestors wore costumes fashioned from gold-encrusted silks and gauzes, and topped by a hat curiously reminiscent of the broad-brimmed headgear worn by Australian troops in the First World War. This kind of dress is no longer worn except during a part of the coronation rites. For trips up-country, the King often dresses informally in a safari suit, or trousers and bush shirt. For public appearances in Bangkok—when the King attends a royal cremation, for example, or presides at troop reviews, pays respect to his forebears in the Royal Pantheon, or changes the vestments of the Emerald Buddha—he favours the white, high-collared uniform and gold-braided, peaked hat of Thai officialdom.

Still, many reminders of bygone pageantry catch the eye on such occasions. His household attendants wear traditional blue and white livery, and one of them carries a gigantic flat-topped umbrella that symbolizes royalty. When the King is required to be seated, a vertical yellow banner emblazoned with a red *garuda*—a mythical bird-man—is hung on the wall behind the gilded seat that does duty as a throne, and a table is furnished with a gilded stand containing two tumblers of water, augmented on very formal occasions by golden utensils for preparing betel nut, a mild stimulant once very common but seldom chewed by urban Thais these days.

Often during royal ceremonies the King sits impassively for hours on

Two of Bangkok's most sacred monuments, the Emerald Buddha (above) and the spire-topped wooden post (right) called Lak Muang—believed to house the guardian spirit of the city—were both set up by Rama I when he founded the new capital in 1782. The 23-inch-high Emerald Buddha, actually carved from a solid piece of green jade by Thai craftsmen in the 14th Century or earlier, sits on an altar in its own temple in the grounds of the Grand Palace. Half a mile to the south-east stands the Lak Muang shrine, visited by a ceaseless stream of petitioners who paste gold leaf on the post in the hope of being granted a private wish.

end, sometimes flanked by his warmly smiling Queen and always backed by rows of solemn dignitaries clad in white and gold uniforms with an astonishing array of medal ribbons on each distinguished breast. Most time-consuming of all are the graduation ceremonies at Bangkok's major universities. The King bestows the certificates with his own hand, and so many students graduate every year that, by the time each one has advanced and retired with the requisite bows and curtseys, the ceremony will have lasted up to four days.

The King and other senior members of the royal family also attend a great number of fund-raising ceremonies for various worthy purposes. Each donor has the honour of being presented and of personally handing over a cheque, enclosed in a white envelope resting on a gilded offering-tray with a vase-like stem. In return, he or she may receive a small medallion as a token of esteem from the royal hand. The merit thus acquired and the pride and pleasure that go with it are a sure way of eliciting generous donations from the public.

Since 1932, the powers of the Thai king have been no greater than those normally enjoyed by constitutional monarchs in the modern world, but his influence in politics has been much greater. Under the constitution he is accorded the prerogatives to be consulted in political matters by any of his subjects, to give advice and to offer encouragement. King Bhumibol has regularly exercised all three. During the political upheaval of 1973, he granted several audiences to student leaders and, while supporting their desire for democracy, advised them to give up violence as a means to that end. He also advised the leaders of the military regime, Thanom Kittikachorn and Prapass Charusathiara, to go into exile in the interests of political stability. They did so, opening the way, ironically, for three years of increasingly unstable, if democratic, government.

The King's role in the nightmarish politics of 1976 is more controversial. The true story of the events leading to the massacre of students at Thammasat University and the military coup of October 6 will probably never be fully known. Some observers have suggested that the King, worried about the instability of the government and the danger of Communist subversion, may have hesitated to use his influence in an attempt to forestall the competing military factions. There is good reason to think he was deeply shocked by the killings at the Thammasat campus, but he was prepared to acquiesce in the ending of parliamentary democracy and is believed to have suggested the appointment of a civilian, Thanin Kraivichien, as the new Prime Minister. In the event, Thanin held power for only one year, but the King's ability to influence political decisions had been demonstrated once more.

Since 1976, leftist groups in exile have been denigrating the King in secretly distributed leaflets and clandestine radio programmes. But within Thailand there is still strong support for the monarchy. The attitudes of

Beneath the stone statue of a Chinese warrior in the precincts of Wat Po, members of the Thai Boy Scouts and its sister movement, the Girl Guides, receive a marching lesson from a soldier. Both organizations stress loyalty to the monarchy, and the King and Queen serve respectively as their honorary patrons.

people in Bangkok and in the kingdom as a whole cannot be understood without realizing that discontent with whatever political regime is in power by no means implies disloyalty to the House of Chakri. In a country subject to frequent changes of government by *coups d'état*, many Thais see the monarchy as the perpetual symbol and safeguard of their national values.

The national slogan, originally adopted by the People's Party of 1932 and frequently employed by governments since, is "For Nation, Religion and King". Nationalism used to be a concept quite foreign to the Thais and, in the early years of this century, King Vajiravudh laboured with scant success to instil it in his people. Through recent external pressures—the toppling of the Laotian monarchy after the Vietnam War, the near destruction of the Buddhist religion there, and Communist excesses in Cambodia —it would seem that the spirit of nationalism has become more widely inculcated. But behind it lies the much more ancient concept of a people led by a divine monarch whose radiance emanates from a capital city.

Despite all the changes of the last hundred years, Bangkok is still in a very real sense a City of Deities. Its fortunes remain under the protection of the Emerald Buddha. When Laos turned Communist, some Laotians demanded the return of the statue to Vientiane, whence General Chakri, Rama I-to-be, had removed it 200 years before; but Thais would as soon think of surrendering their country as of handing over this embodiment of their identity. Equally important as protectors of the city's fortunes are the Lak Muang deity, enshrined close to the Grand Palace, and the King himself, upholder of a tradition that has lasted for 700 years. Were any of these to suffer eclipse, most Thais would take it as a dreadful omen.

The Glory of the Chakri Kings

Behind the crenellated wall of the Grand Palace complex, fluted towers signifying a royal founder punctuate Wat Phra Keo's panorama of roofs and spires.

Shimmering amid the tangled cityscape, Bangkok's Buddhist *wats*—temple complexes usually incorporating a monastery—mesmerize the eye with their glazed roofs, obelisk-like towers (*prangs*) and graceful spires (*chedis*). Of the 400-odd wats, the most spectacular—pictured on this and the following pages—proclaim not only the pre-eminence of Buddhism but also the glory of the Chakri kings who built them. The noblest of all, Wat Phra Keo (above), stands within the Grand Palace precincts but includes no monastery, since tradition forbids monks to inhabit royal residences. It was built by King Rama I in 1785 to house the Emerald Buddha, a medieval figure made of green jade and now prized as Thailand's greatest treasure (*page 90*). Later kings followed his example at other sites, enriching their city's beauty while adding to their personal store of religious merit.

Tiles on the tiered roofs of temple buildings at Wat Phra Keo are glazed in red and green and closely laid to overlap in a net-like pattern.

Dwarfed by a gilded chedi, a monument at Wat Phra Keo holds King Mongkut's crown. Bronze statues of royal white elephants stand guard.

Monkey warriors, supporting a section of façade at Wat Arun, honour the Buddha with an exultant dance.

A mosaic of fragmented porcelain, donated at royal request by Rama III's subjects and arranged to represent flowers and leaves, spangles this chedi at Wat Arun.

The gilded Buddha at Wat Benchamabopit, framed by softly lit columns made of Italian marble, contains ashes of the wat's founder, King Chulalongkorn.

4

Legions of the Faithful

Every day, the brightening of the sky that heralds the sudden upsurge of dawn brings to Bangkok's streets a colourful spectacle. From the city's 400-odd wats emerge streams of shaven-headed Buddhist monks wearing saffron robes. In dignified silence, they pass lightly from house to house, graciously accepting the food offerings provided by the faithful—pious householders who stand ready at their doorways to ladle out large spoonfuls of rice, curry or some other cooked food wrapped in banana leaves, or more commonly in plastic, and perhaps some sweets or fruit.

According to the ancient rules of their faith, the monks are permitted to own nothing other than their robes, their metal food bowls and four other bare essentials: a razor, a needle and some thread for repairing the robes, a girdle to secure the under-robe, and a strainer through which to pour their drinking water. The strainer is intended to prevent them from swallowing any insects that may be in the water, since the Buddhist concern for preserving life extends to all creatures. Monks nowadays may also have a few other personal effects such as a cup and saucer, an umbrella, a pillow and simple footwear; but, being forbidden so much as to touch money, they rely on donations for all their everyday necessities. The reason they set out so early each morning is that the two meals a day to which they are restricted must be eaten before noon. The first is taken when they return to the wat at about 7 o'clock and the second, consisting of leftovers, at about 11. During the rest of the day, which they devote to contemplation, study, liturgical rites and relaxation, only liquids may pass their lips.

It would be quite wrong to describe the monks' early morning round as begging. On the contrary, the reverential expressions and gestures of the donors are those of people taking part in a religious rite. They make their offerings with as much respect as would be accorded to royalty. The donors believe that by supporting the Sangha, or sacred brotherhood of Buddhist monks, they will be rewarded by a store of merit—a gain that far outweighs the value of the offerings and the trouble of preparing them at such an early hour.

Merit-making of a more lavish kind is ritualized in the annual *kathin* or robe-offering ceremonies that start at the end of the rainy season in mid-October and last for about one month. On these occasions, donors provide new robes and a variety of other gifts to see the brotherhood through the coming year: foodstuffs, utensils, cleaning materials and money for the upkeep of the temple, as well as a few special items such as a new altar table or an electric fan. Money for the gifts to each wat is

Holding flowers and incense sticks, solemn-faced soldiers take part in ceremonies marking Visakha Bucha, the annual festival of the birth, Enlightenment and death of the Buddha—all said to have occurred the same day of the year. Visakha Bucha is celebrated as one of Thailand's most important national holidays, a reminder that 90 per cent of Thais are Buddhists.

raised under the sponsorship of a school, or a government department, a wealthy family or a group of well-wishers. Then, on a day agreed with the abbot, the donors take their offerings through the streets to the wat.

In the central districts of Bangkok most *kathin* groups nowadays travel by car, but in the quiet suburbs one may see traditional *kathin* processions led by colourfully dressed men and women dancing joyously to the rhythm of long, cone-like drums. Behind the dancers come donors bearing trays of saffron robes and household necessities, quite often unabashedly bedecked with rolls of coloured toilet paper. Some carry artificial trees whose foliage consists of banknotes wedged in slots cut in the branches. The money will be used by the wat's lay guardians as needs arise.

The grandest procession is the royal water-borne *kathin*, held on a day decided by the palace. Ever since the foundation of Bangkok, the king has annually visited one or more royal temples, often travelling by state barge. On such an occasion, he starts out from the royal landing stage on the east bank of the Chao Phya River, close to the Grand Palace. Enthroned in the middle of a gilded craft, propelled by 40 oarsmen wearing collarless jackets and narrow calf-length trousers of scarlet cloth, he proceeds over the water to the sound of the oarsmen's rhythmic chanting and the beat of drums, followed by other state barges carrying members of the royal family, courtiers, and gifts for the monks.

At various times of the year, some wats organize fund-raising fairs, usually in aid of a project to construct or renovate a temple building. With money given by regular supporters, the wat hires bands to play in the outer precincts of the temple complex and encourages itinerant food-sellers to come and set up their stalls. Known friends of the wat are invited to attend recitations of the Buddhist scriptures and to contribute generously to the project. Other people come from many parts of the city to enjoy the fair, and most of these visitors present a sum of money to the lay bursar of the wat before they leave.

In their present-day form, the fund-raising fairs are, in my opinion, the least attractive of temple functions. As recently as the 1950s and 1960s, they afforded opportunities to see a variety of exotic stage shows—perhaps five or six at a large wat—performed on bamboo platforms lit by naphtha flares. Participants in Thai *likay*—traditional musical plays with an all-female cast and romantic or heroic themes—sang their parts at the tops of their voices, supported by a cacophony of ancient instruments. Simultaneously, on other platforms only a few yards away, actors in perhaps two different Chinese opera performances launched into their astonishingly high-pitched arias with an ear-splitting accompaniment of gongs and cymbals and the piercing notes of two-stringed fiddles. Today, the harsh electric lights that have replaced the flares reveal the tawdriness of the costumes and dispel much of the mystery. Worse still, the powerful amplifiers used by all the performing companies—and by the growing

Aided by youngsters, a Buddhist monk (top, right) returns to his wat with morning food donations provided by households in one of Bangkok's outlying districts. Since many of the city's commuting workers do not have time to prepare morning food offerings, they may make merit instead by paying for meals, lotus buds and incense sticks that monks can pick up at bus station food-stalls (below, right).

number of Thai and Western-style pop bands that now draw the largest crowds at the fairs—create a din that is no longer amusing but unbearable.

One feature of the fairs that has not changed is the large number of stalls dispensing a hundred kinds of spicy snacks. It is as well that the monks themselves do not venture into the part of the fairground where these stalls are set up; the foods create a great thirst among the throng of fair-goers, who appease it with generous quantities of beer and spirits distilled from rice. Drunkenness within the grounds of a temple may seem mildly shocking, but the monks, while keeping their distance, exhibit a kindly tolerance of other people's enjoyments

Activities in support of the sacred Sangha are willingly performed by all Bangkok's lay Buddhists—which is to say, the vast majority of the city's population. They greatly prize the merit they accumulate, but in a very different way from a devout Christian, who may set store by virtuous behaviour as a means of finding favour with God. The form of Buddhism almost universally practised in Thailand—Theravada—is a religion that dispenses with the very concept of God. At the heart of the doctrine—and very much in the minds of all Thai Buddhists—is the idea that a stockpile of merit ensures future life at a higher level of existence than before. This notion is drawn from the belief, also central to Hinduism, in a long succession of rebirths.

The Buddha himself was born in India and knew the religion of the Brahman priests, who strongly influenced the development of Hinduism. Named Siddhartha Gautama, he grew up as a member of India's princely caste at the end of the 6th Century B.C. Overwhelmed, at the age of 29, with a sense that "all human life is suffering", he renounced his life of ease, abandoned his wife and family, and set out on a quest for truth that led eventually to the profound intuitive experience called "Enlightenment". (The term "Buddha" actually means "Enlightened One".) His subsequent life was spent preaching to others about what he had discovered.

Dismissing questions about the ultimate meaning of the universe as idly speculative, the Buddha taught his disciples to overcome their earthly nature, with all its attendant evils, and to attain an imperturbable tranquillity by the practice of wisdom and compassion. Existence, he proclaimed, inevitably involves suffering, bereavement, sickness and death. Driven by the three fires of evil—passion, delusion and inordinate desire (or its opposite, aversion)—all sentient beings forge chains of *karma*, a determining influence that arises from their actions for good or evil in one life and will decide their fate in the next. Briefly and simply stated, this doctrine asserts that as long as *karma* continues to be generated, beings must endure aeon upon aeon of rebirth, each time in a higher or lower form of existence. (A gross accumulation of evil deeds may even cause a human being to be reborn in animal form.) However, by relinquishing all

A monk who acts as gatekeeper at Wat Saket, one of the largest and wealthiest wats in Bangkok, chats cheerfully on the phone amid a cosy clutter of cushions, flowers, framed portraits of members of the royal family and other personal effects. At most monasteries, monks live in more spartan conditions, with a minimum of private possessions.

personal desire and by ridding himself of the illusion of his individuality, man can release himself from *karma*-forming tendencies and, after many lifetimes of endeavour, thereby attain *nirvana*—the blessing of total liberation that transcends both life and death.

For a Thai, the most merit-worthy action, and thus the best way of working towards this ultimate goal, is to join the monkhood. Some monks remain in a monastery for many years or even a lifetime, but all are free to return to lay life whenever they wish. Most Thai males, from the king downwards, take the saffron robe for a short period at some stage of their lives, usually in their early twenties before they have family responsibilities to fulfil. The temporary commitment, usually lasting from a few weeks to a few months, is regarded as a preparation for adulthood and also confers merit on other members of the monk's family, especially the women—who cannot join the Sangha. By undergoing the discipline of monastic life before marriage, a young man gains merit for his parents and so repays a debt of gratitude for his upbringing. After marriage, a portion of the merit he gains is thought to be conferred on his wife.

Most Thais elect to join the monkhood during the Buddhist Lent, which coincides with the rainy months of the year when work on the land more or less stops and employment of other sorts may be difficult to obtain. In June, when the rainy season is just about to start, one sometimes sees processions of young men going to the temples for ordination. Dressed in white robes, the ordinands sit solemnly in cars decorated with garlands of flowers. Not too many years ago they would have ridden to the wat on horseback in emulation of the Buddha when, as Prince Gautama, he renounced the luxury of palace life and rode away on his white horse to study under spiritual teachers and learn the art of meditation.

The way of life to which the monks will be dedicating themselves— whether for years or only months or weeks—is one of scrupulous self-control. Their day-to-day behaviour is circumscribed by no less than 227 monastic rules (recited every full moon to ensure that they have been committed to memory). They must abjure all frivolous entertainments such as the cinema and television. To preserve chastity, they must avoid the least occasion for temptation: gifts from women are received on a square of cloth laid on the ground, so as to avert any accidental brushing of fingers; and monks travelling on Bangkok's crowded buses (which they do free of charge) take care not even to be touched by a woman's garments. These customs may seem unnecessarily strict, but the aim is to preclude any possibility of gossip that might harm the good name of the sacred Sangha.

The communities of monks in the wats range from a mere dozen to several hundred. Some monks are housed in dormitories, others in tiny one-room buildings that are ideal for a life of meditation. These quarters are usually clearly separated from that section of the wat in which public ceremonies take place.

During a fund-raising ceremony at Wat Mahatat, people gather to be blessed by a monk seated beneath a tree, or to burn joss sticks at the outdoor shrines. Monasteries are maintained almost entirely by the private donations made at such ceremonies or during fairs that lure crowds with entertainments and feasting.

At one time the most sacred part of every Buddhist temple used to be a tall reliquary tower—either a pointed *chedi* or a *prang* with its rounded top—containing the ashes of venerated monks. The tower was surrounded by a cloister with a chapel at each of the four main compass points. In these chapels were housed statues representing the four chief events in the Buddha's life—his birth, Enlightenment, first sermon and final passing into *nirvana*. This arrangement is still common in Bangkok, but in many of the city's temples nowadays the most sacred part is a large assembly hall known as a *bot*, whose interior is dominated by a statue of the Buddha. A *bot* is generally rectangular and contains space for many monks. It is divided into three aisles by rows of columns that support vermilion-painted roofs decorated in gold.

A typical wat complex includes several other sacred buildings. There may be a *viharn*, or lofty hall, where laymen attend religious ceremonies; subsidiary *chedis*; open-sided pavilions to shelter visitors from sun and rain; temple-like crematoria; and several mortuary chapels for the use of bereaved families during obsequies. There is also likely to be a *mondop*, a curious pillared loft for storing objects of veneration; these will almost certainly include hundreds of pressed palm-leaf volumes containing the entire Buddhist scriptures in Pali, the ancient Indo-Aryan language that has been the canonical tongue of Buddhism since the 1st Century B.C. This massive work, the Tipitaka, has been translated into Thai and printed in 80 volumes with pages of the thinnest paper for the benefit of anyone whose knowledge of Pali is deficient—and that includes many of the monks, especially the temporary members of the brotherhood.

During festivals and on the four holy days of the lunar month that correspond with the phases of the moon, the wats are crowded with people who have come with food for the monks and to make temple offerings of flowers, candles, incense sticks and gold leaf. At times they may be seen sitting on the floor of the *viharn*, legs tucked respectfully behind them, listening to a sermon preached by a monk sitting cross-legged on the Buddhist equivalent of a pulpit—a cushioned, throne-like chair decorated with gilded wood-carving inset with fragments of stained glass.

On Visakha Bucha, the full-moon night of May, the city celebrates the birth, Enlightenment and passing into *nirvana* of the Buddha (according to tradition, all three events, though separated in time, are supposed to have taken place on the same day of the year). Crowds stream to the temples after sunset and it is beautiful to see processions of men, women and children three times circling the *bots* in the temple compounds. Each person carries a lighted candle and sticks of incense. From a distance, the worshippers look like a vast swarm of fireflies sweeping round and round a brilliantly moonlit building. Seen from still further away, the glittering lights merge to form a chain of yellowish-white fire. Before the ritual circling starts, the people pledge themselves to observe the

Against the background of a modern shopping complex, a Buddhist nun's handwritten account of ill health and misfortune invites passers-by to contribute to her medical bills. Far less numerous than monks and not recognized as full members of the monastic community, nuns —known as "chi"—are usually devout elderly women who perform menial tasks in wats.

voluntary undertakings which, in Buddhism, replace the Ten Command-ments of Judaism and Christianity. Chorusing the Pali syllables, they promise to abstain from killing, stealing, improper sexual intercourse, lying and imbibing "sloth-producing intoxicants".

These pledges are solemnly undertaken, but one or two—especially the restrictions on sex and drink—may be difficult to observe for long. With typical pragmatism, therefore, the Thais sometimes mentally stipulate a brief time-limit for such promises—a practice that has prompted one writer to remark, memorably if unkindly, that in Thailand adultery is practised on alternate days.

That the easy-going and hedonistic people of Bangkok, apparently care-free in matters of religion, should subscribe at all—and in all sincerity—to such an other-worldly doctrine as Buddhism seems on the surface to be highly paradoxical. Yet, the very detachment of Buddhism acts as a perfect complement to the worldliness of the Thais. I recall how Luang Charas, a colleague of mine at Chulalongkorn University, replied to an American sociologist who had unwisely spoken of the monks as "a useless drain upon the wealth of the community".

"Ridiculous," cried the old gentleman, for once goaded out of his cheerful good manners. "Our debt to the Sangha is out of all proportion to the little it costs us to provide for them. They are society's greatest asset. By relieving them from mundane worries so that they can devote their time to inward cultivation, we provide ourselves with a spiritual reservoir of tremendous value to the nation. Their presence among us diminishes the evil *karma* by which any city is bound. They are our spiritual guardians, and all who contribute to their upkeep share in their merit." Coming from a generally light-hearted man, these words made a great impression on me.

Moreover, the Thais see no division between the spiritual and material worlds. Such a division—a Christian concept—is quite foreign to them. Buddhists see all phenomena as manifestations of a fundamentally unchanging reality, which is neither spirit as opposed to matter nor matter as opposed to spirit. Mystics who proclaim that there is no real difference between dung and ambrosia, spittle and nectar, come closest to expressing what the Thais, without bothering their heads about it, intuitively feel to be the nature of existence. Thus sincere piety may go hand in hand with a great capacity for the enjoyment of sensual pleasure. To the Thais, the equation of pleasure with sinfulness seems incomprehensible. They feel that precisely because life is so often frustrating and unsatisfactory, one should make the most of any enjoyments that happen to come one's way; and they act accordingly.

What they abhor as altogether evil is any deliberate attempt to harm other people, mentally or physically. For instance the Buddhist precept against improper sexual intercourse is often taken to mean that sexual

The Faces of Buddha

After 800 years of Buddhist influence, Thailand may have more images of Buddha than it has human inhabitants. In theory, all of the representations should carry a sacred sameness: the images have a common source—the ancient texts describing the Enlightened One; and all are intended by their anonymous creators to embody the spirit of the Lord Buddha's teachings. In practice, however, the Buddha shows many faces to Thai believers. Interpretations range from a Buddha emaciated by fasting (top row, left) to the serene tranquillity of the figure shown next to it—both examples of a style that prevailed six centuries ago.

Most of Bangkok's temple Buddhas are made of bronze, although some—like the Wat Trimitr image (bottom row, centre) have been encrusted with gold leaf by generations of devotees. A few are made of solid gold, such as Wat Trimitr's more famous Golden Buddha (middle row, right). Cast from $5\frac{1}{2}$ tons of the precious metal in the 13th or 14th Century, it was later coated in plaster to conceal its value from Burmese invaders. In this disguise, the image remained little noticed until 1953, when a crane moving the Buddha to another building accidentally damaged the plaster, exposing the un-dimmed gold beneath.

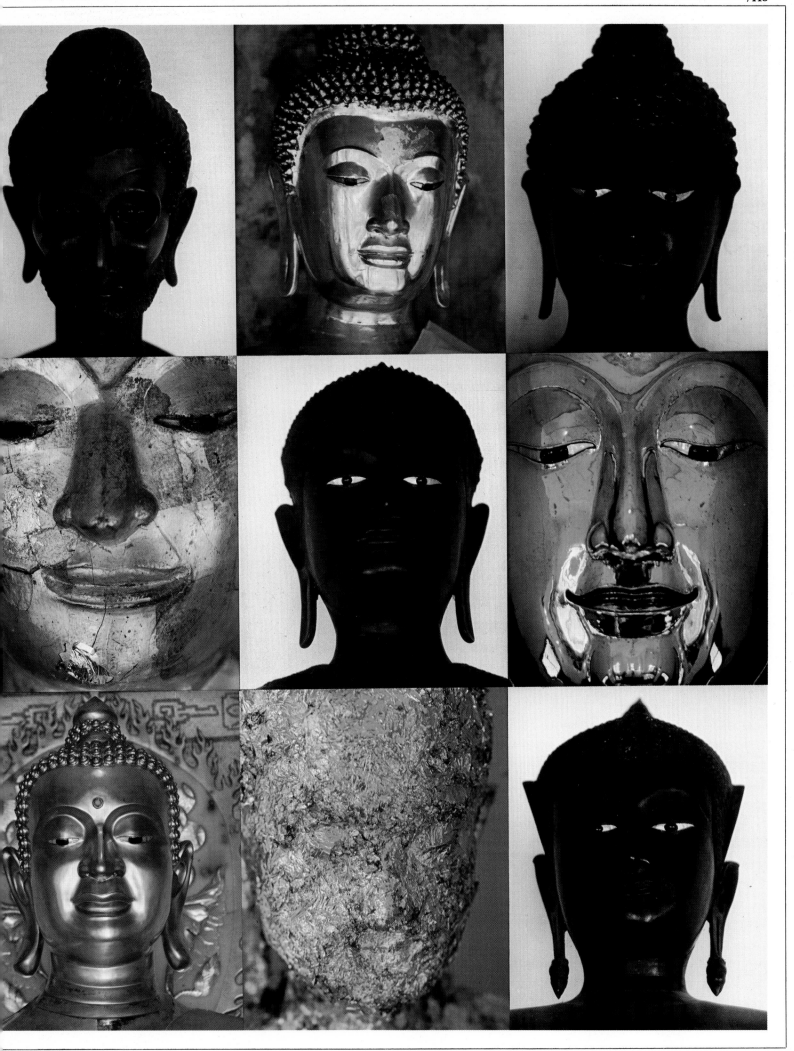

enjoyment becomes wrong only when it causes suffering—perhaps to a third person, such as the spouse of one of the participants or a fond parent. In that sense the rule is for the most part strictly observed. And although many ugly crimes are committed and avidly reported in the more sensational sections of the press, premeditated murders are comparatively rare in Bangkok. Except in moments of blind anger, Thais adhere closely to the precept against killing any living being. Until the late 1950s the municipality could not even bring itself to arrange for the rounding up and destruction of stray dogs and cats, though hordes used to roam the city's byways. When eventually the authorities took action, they justified it by the argument that they were reducing the suffering of starving, disease-ridden animals. Even now, householders often take unwanted litters of puppies or kittens to a monastery compound, where they stealthily release them rather than dispose of them at home; the monks can be counted on to feed these poor creatures with leftover offerings. A corollary to this revulsion against taking life is the belief that it is meritorious to rescue doomed creatures; at temple festivals one may see caged birds being bought by worshippers and then let loose into the air, or captive fish and turtles set free in canals or ponds.

A second, and perhaps more genuine, paradox is that while the Thais subscribe to a doctrine which does not admit the existence of God as the Creator and instead stresses self-endeavour, self-development and self-salvation, they nevertheless make offerings to a whole pantheon of gods and spirits. The Thais cannot help regretting that Buddhism offers no guidance in such important everyday matters as forecasting the results of the next state lottery, putting through a successful business deal or increasing a woman's fertility, and that it provides no special rituals for weddings, coronations or similar rites. For all such needs, they find themselves turning to other religious traditions: rituals and deities of Hindu origin, inherited from medieval times when Cambodian influence was paramount; and nature gods whose worship survives from the time more than nine centuries ago when the Thais' own ancestors still lived among the mountain fastnesses of south China.

An admirable aspect of this religious flexibility is the willingness of the Thais to allow other peoples freedom of worship. The national tolerance was well illustrated a century ago by King Mongkut's generosity towards Christian missionaries whose express design was to wean his subjects away from their Buddhist faith. When the missionaries asked for a centre from which to conduct what to this pious monarch must have seemed like a nefarious activity, he unhesitatingly made over to them part of a Buddhist temple. Due largely to such broadmindedness on the part of the Chakri monarchs, Bangkok has long abounded in heterogeneous places of worship. There are Chinese temples, both Buddhist and non-Buddhist; Vietnamese temples; mosques for Thai Muslims; Hindu temples for the

Birth of a Sage

Manufacturing images of the Buddha is big business in Bangkok. In addition to supplying statues for temples and home shrines throughout Thailand, local factories export to Japan, Malaysia and other countries where Buddhism is extensively practised.

Small Buddha figures, made of plaster, are mass-produced; but any large image—such as those shown here—begins as an individually sculpted wax model that can be used only once. After it has been coated with clay and then surrounded by a supporting metal frame (near right), the wax is melted out, leaving a hollow mould in which a brass Buddha is cast. This image receives a coating of resin (centre) that enables a subsequent covering of gold leaf to stick. The final product (far right) will sell for at least $2,500, but it does not become an object of veneration until it is consecrated by monks.

city's many Indian cloth-merchants, as well as for the small number of Thai Brahmans; there are also Christian schools and churches, of both Catholic and Protestant denominations.

For the eclectic Thais themselves, a large number of shrines are erected all over the city to the deities of various faiths and sects. Even within the precincts of the main Buddhist temples, though always in a subordinate position, are found images of other faiths: for instance, a large *lingam* (phallic symbol) raised to the Hindu god Shiva, who is often worshipped in this form, stands in the compound of Wat Po, the Temple of the Reclining Buddha.

By far the most prestigious shrine in the city is the handsome, open-sided pavilion that stands beside the Erawan Hotel at a traffic-congested intersection in the tourist area of east Bangkok. It houses a gilded statue of the four-headed Hindu deity Brahma. During the hotel's construction in the 1950s several workers were injured in mysterious accidents, and the shrine was erected in propitiation, to prevent further mishaps. However, it soon acquired a reputation for bringing good fortune to all and sundry. Day and night, petitioners crowd about the statue of Brahma, burning incense and candles, and bringing such a profusion of flowers that the attendants have to clear them away every few minutes.

If the suppliant's wishes are granted, he will return soon afterwards to express his gratitude; he may set up several tables in the shrine enclosure and offer the deity an eight- or twelve-course banquet, or else employ

A mould receives a metal frame.

Black resin paint is applied.

Newly made Buddhas await sale.

musicians and a troupe of dancers to perform before the statue. During the rush-hour, perhaps, when the roar and stench of traffic are at their worst, one may see enacted a dance not unlike those witnessed by Louis XIV's ambassadors to the court of Ayutthaya. The fumes of petrol are submerged in the heavy fragrance of incense. The din of cars mingles with the throb of drums and the tinkle of xylophones. The dancers, in gorgeously brocaded costumes, dance on oblivious of all else, their limbs moving with sinuous grace. Yet, the drivers of the vehicles waiting for the traffic-lights to change seldom glance at a spectacle so familiar. Only tourists, noses pressed against the windows of their air-conditioned buses, are struck by the astonishing incongruity.

Much smaller shrines are commonly found in the gardens of private houses or on the roof-tops. Strictly speaking, they should be placed where the shadow of a building will never fall on them; otherwise, it is thought, their efficacy will be impaired. Perched on slim pillars, they range from what look like wooden dovecotes to magnificent replicas of Thai or Cambodian temples made of painted stone or plaster. These shrines house the tutelary, or protective, deities of the home, which are usually represented by gilded wooden tablets, whereas their sacred consorts and attendant elephants appear in the form of clay images, crudely fashioned but not without charm. Not to provide a shrine to the tutelary deity of one's dwelling is to court disaster, but it is considered even more risky to have one and then fail to look after it, or to be careless about making daily offerings of incense and flowers.

Once, after my manservant had sustained a severe head injury and I had been so badly stung by a poisonous insect that my face swelled to almost twice its normal size, my neighbours urged me to have the dilapidated wooden shrine at the bottom of my garden replaced, "lest worse befall". I could not find an expert in the delicate art of persuading a tutelary deity to move house, so my housekeeper engaged the services of a Chinese medium who assured her he could summon a spirit to perform the task.

A new shrine was carefully erected beside the old one. In front of it was placed a table laden with a pig's head, a roast chicken and three cups of powerful rice spirit. After seeing to these preparations, the medium entered a state of trance and, waving a sword above his head, began to speak in the unearthly accents of the spirit he had summoned to possess him, calling on the tutelary deity to condescend to take up his new abode. Pausing long enough for this deity to inhale the essence of the pig's head, chicken and wine, we then set about obliterating his former shrine by burning both it and its supporting pillar, burying the ashes deep in the ground and then smoothing over the earth so that not a trace of it remained. This done, the medium and my household were free to enjoy the earthly husks of the feast from which the deity had already abstracted the vital elements. My manservant and I presently recovered, and all was well.

A small boy frolics in a shop display of garden furniture that includes elaborately carved and gilded spirit houses. These expensive miniature temples will serve their purchasers as status objects, as well as providing suitable shelter for the guardian spirits of the property.

Manoeuvring darkly behind the numerous gods and guardian spirits of the Thai pantheon are all manner of ghosts and demons, many of them malevolent. The ghosts of people who have met violent and untimely ends are believed to develop a voracious appetite for dragging others to the same doom. They were alleged to be the cause of the mysterious deaths of construction workers at the Erawan Hotel, of a succession of fatal car accidents suffered by officials of the United Nations Organization in Bangkok when I worked there a number of years ago, and of many another grisly mishap.

"Our belief in ghosts is so lively," a woman colleague of mine at Chulalongkorn University once admitted ruefully, "that our children constantly hear stories fit to scare them out of their wits; and an unusual noise in the night makes even grown-ups duck their heads under the bedclothes. I know it's silly, but you won't catch me voicing my disbelief in ghosts after dark, especially if the dogs have sensed their presence. I am a Thai, after all. Knowing our weaknesses is one thing; not sharing them is quite another."

So pervasive in Bangkok are beliefs in supernatural agencies that many people refuse to start a journey without consulting their stars. There are men who hold degrees from noted universities in Europe and America who pride themselves on their expert knowledge of the ancient mysteries of astrology. Serious cabinet decisions may be made to conform with planetary conjunctions, and a recent Prime Minister was himself an eminent astrologer—no doubt a great convenience when decisions had to be made in a hurry.

After living here for a while, even foreigners cease to be overly sceptical towards supernatural phenomena. I believe few long-term residents of Bangkok would take up a challenge to wander about their houses during the dark and silent hours before dawn, daring ghosts and demons to do their worst. Nevertheless, the more benevolent spirits may be used to good advantage. To contact them, of course, requires the services of a medium. Both Thai and Chinese mediums may be consulted; but I myself have found the performances by the Chinese the more dramatic.

Perhaps one visits a gnarled old peasant whose whole appearance suggests that he could scarcely write his own name. Deeply entranced, body shaking, eyes vacant, saliva dribbling down his chin, his right arm (which wields a willowwood baton) jerking spasmodically, he sits with a scribe beside him before a tray of sand. Suppliants kneel in front of him and one of them asks a question, perhaps whether a long-suffered illness can be cured, a lost love regained or a business transaction concluded.

Suddenly the movements of the medium's arm become more violent and the point of the baton is brought down into the loose sand, where it traces rapidly the complicated characters of a four-line Chinese poem—20 or 28 characters in all. As they appear, the scribe hurriedly records them, then reads out the poem. I myself have several times addressed a question to this kind of "oracle", framing it in such a way as to give no clue to the answer desired. On each occasion the response has disturbingly revealed what seems like an intimate knowledge of my private concerns. How to account for such prescience I do not know.

Such men have great influence and appeal in Bangkok, but I do not share the view expressed by some people that Buddhism in the city has been almost lost amid extraneous superstitions, any more than I find that it is likely to be swamped by Westernization. Even those Thais who are most prone to seek help from the pantheon of assorted gods and spirits are aware, I think, that man's chief enemy, his own egoism, cannot be conquered by supernatural aid; and while, on the other hand, there are many Thais today who rarely visit a Buddhist temple except to attend the obsequies of relatives and friends, they still adhere to the fundamental principles of their religion.

Buddhism, after all, has over the centuries profoundly modified the Thai character; and it continues to be a prime source of conscious and unconscious motivation. It certainly helps to explain why Thais are a kinder, happier and more tolerant people than most—qualities that the pressure of modern urban life must place under increasing strain. If there are paradoxes in the religious lives of the Thais—the tension between the teachings of the Buddha and the array of practical gods adopted from other cultures, between piety and sensuality, between faith and Western materialism—these are resolved, on closer acquaintance, by the very Buddhist belief that diversity is in the end an illusion that will be transcended with the dawning of Enlightenment.

Joining the Sacred Brotherhood

The candidate's mother cuts the first lock of his hair at the start of the ceremony, watched by relatives who will each take a turn with the scissors.

Thai ceremonies typically involve a blend of high spirits and deep religious feeling—and none more so than the ordination ceremony by which men are inducted into the Buddhist monkhood. A spell of a few weeks or months in a wat is believed to confer great merit, not only on the monk himself, but also on his family (particularly his mother) and on all his friends and neighbours. Thus, the ordination ritual, known as a *buat naag,*

attracts crowds of well-wishers who turn the proceedings into a joyful festival, with the candidate as the hero of the occasion. Most men do their monastic service between the ages of 20 and 25. Some who are especially devout re-enter the wat for a period of spiritual refreshment later in their careers—a merit-making path chosen by the department store owner whose *buat naag* at Wat Saket is pictured on these pages.

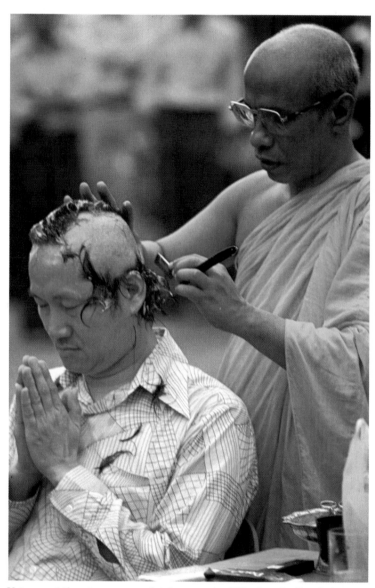

Using a cut-throat razor, a monk takes over the difficult task of head-shaving.

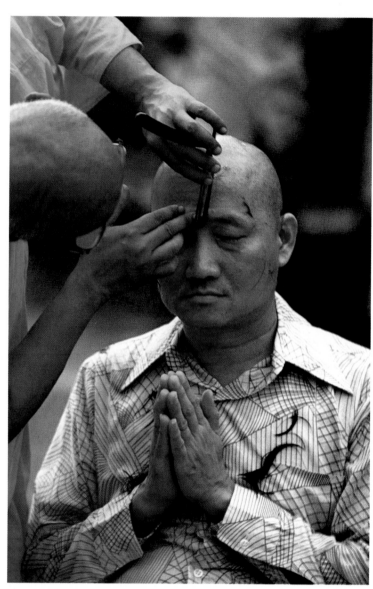

The candidate preserves his composure as the monk tackles his eyebrows.

A Symbolic Cleansing

The ritual shaving by family and friends that begins the *buat naag* will be completed by a monk—himself perhaps a relative or friend of the candidate. Then, eyebrows are removed and fingernails pared: like hair, they symbolize the impermanent things of this world. After a final purification (opposite), the candidate prostrates himself before a shrine dedicated to the monastery's guardian spirit, and pronounces his intention to become a resident monk.

An elderly guest at the ceremony uses a silver bowl to rinse the ordinand's head with holy water containing white blossoms. Their colour is a symbol of purity.

Carrying lotus blossoms that symbolize Enlightenment, the solemn candidate continues the ordination rites by joining in a procession three times around t

t, the sacred centre of the monastery—once to honour the Buddha, a second time to honour Sacred Law, and a third time to honour the monastic order.

Costumed girls in the procession bring gifts of household goods for the monks.

Professional dancers, including young men in make-up with red flowers in their hair, animate the procession around the bot with jubilant finger gestures.

Before entering the bot for the final stages of the ordination, the candidate renounces the world by throwing coins and flowers to friends and well-wishers.

Deep in thought, the candidate allows monks to clothe him in his new robe.

Alms bowl slung on his back, the candidate approaches monks who will complete the ordination by questioning him in Pali, the canonical language of Buddhism.

5

The Chinese Connection

Nearly 700 years ago Ramkhamhaeng, one of the earliest Thai monarchs, invited Chinese artisans into the kingdom of Sukhothai to establish a pottery works, which soon became famous for the high quality of its wares. Although Chinese traders had been visiting Sukhothai since its foundation in the mid-13th Century, this was the first Chinese enterprise known to have been set up on Thai soil. Its establishment was a symbolic event, marking the readiness of Thai rulers to welcome alien settlers who had some special contribution to make to the life of the kingdom.

From that time on, the Thais and the Chinese built up an increasingly close relationship. At an official level, the two peoples exchanged formal visits in appropriate manner: for at least 500 years, the Thais periodically sent tribute missions to China, bearing gifts for the emperors and acknowledging their role as overlords of South-East Asia. This feudal obeisance, while pleasing to the emperors, in practice confirmed the autonomy of successive Thai kingdoms (as well as giving Thai royalty an opportunity to do a bit of trading in luxury goods from China). The Chinese for their part despatched emissaries, who were often very favourably received by the Thais—especially, it seems, by the Thai women. One envoy in the 15th Century, Fei Hsin, reported that "whenever [a Thai woman] meets a Chinese man, she is greatly pleased with him and will inevitably prepare wine to entertain and show respect to him, merrily singing and keeping him overnight". Such stories did their bit in encouraging trade and emigration from China. Moreover, immigrants could easily adjust to an environment where rice and fish were the staple foods, where the climate was benign and the people tolerant. Merchants, craftsmen and labourers came to work, settle and often to marry in Thailand.

By the early 16th Century, there was already a predominantly Chinese quarter in the old Thai capital of Ayutthaya. When Bangkok was founded in 1782, a sizeable Chinese community living on the site of the present Grand Palace had to be moved to what is now the Sampeng district before royal building work could begin. During the late 19th and early 20th Centuries, when European investment and technical innovation led to a rapid development of the Thai economy, the Chinese grew enormously in numbers and influence, and today fully half the people of Bangkok—including the royal family—have at least some Chinese blood.

This ethnic arithmetic is by no means immediately evident in Bangkok. Before the Second World War, traditional differences of dress made it possible to distinguish between the Chinese and the Thais; but nowadays,

Two members of a prestigious riding club prepare to set off on a Sunday morning canter in north-east Bangkok. The riders are Thai, but —in common with many of the city's rich— they have some immediate Chinese forebears.

when casual, Western-style clothes are almost universal, it is often hard to tell them apart. Physically they are very much alike. True, Chinese eyelids are without an epicanthic fold and may vanish from sight when the eyes are fully open; true, the Thai complexion tends to be darker. But these distinctions are no guide where widespread intermarriage has blended the racial stocks. And culturally the Chinese in Thailand have become closely integrated, especially in the last few decades.

Take my own neighbourhood in east Bangkok. Most of the shops, warehouses and small factories that have sprung up around my home during the last 15 years are owned by families of Chinese origin. A few of the very old people still speak Thai poorly and with a strong Chinese accent; but those in their forties and fifties are fully bilingual; and those who are 30 or younger are happier speaking Thai than Chinese, which they do fluently.

In Thailand as a whole the Chinese form no more than about 10 per cent of the population. Their concentration in such great numbers in the capital (and to a lesser extent in some large towns) arises from deep-seated cultural forces. The Thais, with the abundantly fertile plain of the Chao Phya River as the heart of their country, have always made a comparatively good living from agriculture. Easy-going and disdainful of commerce, they sought prestige and security from the old *sakdi na* system of land tenure and social order. They never allowed foreigners to acquire cultivated land.

The Chinese, therefore, had either to turn uncultivated land over to agriculture, which they did to some extent, or else find livelihoods outside farming. Because of the vacuum left by the Thais, they found that

The vaulted ceilings of an unfinished mosque rise like concrete flowers above a swampy tract near New Petchburi Road. More than 100 mosques cater to the spiritual needs of Bangkok's 100,000 Muslims, the second largest religious community in the city.

Emerging from a mosque after prayers, a Muslim observes the Islamic duty of altruism by giving alms to a needy woman. Islam was introduced to Thailand by Arab traders in the 13th Century, and the Muslim community is now well integrated into Thai society.

commerce offered the most fruitful opportunities. It was an occupation ideally suited to their temperament. With their dedication to hard work, their thrift and flair for putting money to good use—attributes born of long hardship in their homeland—they were able to organize themselves into a prosperous trading network. Towns were their natural habitat—especially Bangkok, with its thriving port on the Chao Phya River.

During the 17th and 18th Centuries, the Chinese found a particularly profitable niche acting as middle men in the flourishing rice trade that grew up between Thailand and south China. They bought the rice directly from the Thai growers and transported it to Bangkok, where it was loaded on to the seagoing junks. But what brought the Chinese to their present importance in Bangkok was the transformation of medieval Thailand into a developing nation, a process that began when Sir John Bowring signed his commercial treaty with King Mongkut in 1855.

This Anglo-Thai accord, and the similar treaties concluded soon afterwards with other European powers, all but abolished state monopolies and customs duties. European import-export companies moved in to take advantage of the favourable new trading terms, introducing cheap, mass-produced clothing and other manufactured goods to the Thai market, and exporting chiefly rice and teak. Steam-powered rice-mills and saw-mills sprang up, owned and run by Europeans. Banks were founded to provide Western capital and financial expertise. Later came imports of heavy machinery, railway track and rolling stock, electrical appliances, chemical products and eventually buses and cars—all the technological paraphernalia that were to transform Bangkok into a prosperous modern city.

The growth of trade created numerous opportunities for retailers and wholesalers, clerks and compradors—middle men who knew the markets and could act on behalf of newly arrived Westerners. This was a niche the Chinese were well qualified to fill. In addition, vast numbers of labourers were required to work in the mills, on the docks and on public works stimulated by expansion: canals, railways, roads, government buildings. Since Thailand was then a comparatively underpopulated country, and most of the Thai people were unaccustomed to wage labour (and were already profitably employed in growing rice), the demand could not be met internally. As a result, immigrant labourers poured into Bangkok from China, and in smaller numbers from India, Burma, Malaya, Cambodia and Vietnam.

In the case of the Chinese, the influx was swollen by overpopulation, crop failure and famine in their homeland. Between 1850 and 1860, natural disaster provoked the Taiping Rebellion, a peasant revolution inspired by a somewhat communistic ideology and a hatred for the Manchu dynasty. The rebellion cost more lives than the First World War, shook the dynasty to its foundations, and left further misery and devastation. For millions of Chinese, emigration was the only hope of survival.

Today, as one sits sipping tea with an urbane Chinese businessman in an air-conditioned office in one of Bangkok's high-rise buildings, or perhaps in the garden of an expensive suburban villa, it is hard to imagine that a century ago his great-grandfather probably arrived here as an illiterate peasant fleeing from destitution. Yet, I remember just such a well-dressed, carefully barbered person telling me with pride how the founder of his family's ample fortune disembarked in Bangkok, a deck passenger from the south China port of Swatow, carrying his entire property with him—a blue cloth bundle of patched clothes, a sleeping mat and wooden pillow, an oiled paper umbrella and an earthenware teapot in a quilted basket.

Such immigrants, starting their new life as coolies, hoarded their scanty earnings until they had the tiny amount of capital needed to set up as itinerant pedlars, say, or to rent half a *rai* (about one-fifth of an acre) and go in for market gardening on a very small scale. Seldom did they take a day's holiday or add a slice or two of pork or chicken to their diet of plain boiled rice eaten with a few scraps of vegetable and a little chili in order to make it more palatable.

"You must understand," said my friend, "that people like my great-grandfather shared a vision. They saw their unborn descendants as men with smooth hands and comfortable round bellies who would never experience the hardships their ancestors had for centuries endured. It's a firm Chinese principle, a part of the Confucian ethic, that all of us should struggle to secure for our offspring a better life, more opportunities and a better education than we have had. In this way we repay our debt to the

Behind a street lined with the workshops of Chinese jewellery-makers, impoverished newcomers to the city pan a klong, hoping to find waste particles of gold.

forebears who helped make us what we are. People who don't understand call us money-grabbers. Well, so we may be—but with good reason!"

The children of these first-generation immigrants opened little stalls or shops which, growing bigger, enabled the grandchildren to embark on new enterprises. Cook-shops became inns and inns became hotels; minuscule money-lending concerns became banks; and presently there were Chinese saw-mills, fleets of barges, rice-broking firms, and more. The Chinese increasingly took over the expansion started by Europeans. They were unopposed by the Thais, who remained in their traditional roles as government officials and paddy-farmers. Thus a racial division of labour appeared, the Thais all-powerful in politics and solidly entrenched in agriculture, the Chinese unchallenged in commerce, industry and finance —in short, controlling the economy.

King Mongkut, himself of Chinese lineage on his mother's side, had warmly encouraged Chinese immigration from the 1860s onwards. This far-sighted monarch believed that an infusion of Chinese blood would benefit his people and hasten the modernization of his kingdom. He hoped that Chinese male workers would marry Thai girls and thus pass on qualities of industry and thrift to their children.

What Mongkut seems not to have foreseen is that the Chinese immigrants, with abiding loyalty to their families and ancestral communities, would wish to send back home for girls to marry. Initially, it is true, hardly any Chinese women came to Bangkok. They were banned from leaving by their elders, who wished to keep families together as far as possible. The men mostly left home intending to stay only temporarily in Bangkok, make money and return to marry in China. In the event, many immigrants decided to settle permanently, and about half of these did marry Thai girls; so, for a time, it seemed that Mongkut's policy might be working out. But in the first two decades of the 20th Century, when conditions in China became worse than ever and the elders began to relax their bans, Chinese women started to arrive in significant numbers. Whole groups of relatives began coming, too.

Most of the immigrants to Bangkok came from the area of Kwangtung province around Swatow, which had a regular steamer service to the Thai capital from the 1860s onwards. To most Thais, "Chinese" and "Swatownese" are synonymous. The Swatow dialect has become the lingua franca of all Chinese in Bangkok who are not fluent in Thai, and almost all Chinese words that have become part of the Thai language are pronounced in the Swatow manner. But the common background of this new wave of Chinese only helped to reinforce their instinct for separateness. They became a society within a society, starting their own community organizations, providing their own welfare services, establishing their own schools—and keeping tight control of the new economic infrastructure they had created.

Beside the lavishly decorated doorway of a Chinese cake shop, an inscription advertises special confections for the forthcoming Moon Festival, celebrated annually by Bangkok's Chinese in honour of the Moon Goddess. Within the shop, a boy admires a paper aeroplane that is supposedly capable of flying to the moon.

The Thais began to see this prosperous Chinese community as a set of rapacious fellows, who, by banding together, had appropriated a disproportionate share of the national wealth. The reaction is easy to understand, although in fact the Chinese had not so much taken over existing enterprises as created new ones—to the great advantage of the kingdom. After the 1932 coup, when the Thais became increasingly nationalistic, the authorities began to take firm measures against the Chinese. In 1939 they limited the use of the Chinese language in schools to a few hours each week. By the early 1940s discriminatory laws had been passed reserving to Thai nationals a variety of simple occupations, from hairdressing to the manufacture of bricks. Enforcement was somewhat arbitrary. Once, while having his hair cut, the then Prime Minister, Marshal Phibul, ordered the dismissal of a barber whose accent betrayed his Chinese origin—although there was nothing to tell that the man was not a Thai national. For a while, Chinese businessmen found it politic to appoint Thai army officers to their boards as "advisers"; in return for lending their names to the concerns, these appointees received a share of the profits.

After a change of government in 1944, discriminatory measures were relaxed, but the Communist takeover in China in 1949 ushered in a new era of distrust. The Chinese in Bangkok became politically suspect. Some were nationals of what was now a Communist and possibly hostile state; others, although Thai citizens, were thought likely to feel loyalty for their ancestral homeland in its newly powerful guise. In response to such fears, the Thais restricted immigration to 200 persons of each nationality a year— a measure that affected the Chinese most severely because they were coming in the largest numbers. Throughout the 1950s and 1960s, relations remained strained. Thais were officially encouraged to nurture anti-Chinese sentiments. I remember seeing history essays by university students who had been at school during those years and finding that they included almost identically worded criticisms of Chinese shopkeepers. Such narrowing of opinion indicated the vigour and success with which government propaganda had been disseminated.

In recent years, fortunately, there has been little sign of anti-Chinese feeling. True, the leadership of the banned Communist Party of Thailand is believed to be mainly Chinese. But because most of the Chinese in Thailand are so closely attached to private enterprise, they are now generally reckoned to make a poor breeding-ground for Communists. And, as things have turned out, the People's Republic of China has come to be regarded as a friendly country. The Thais established diplomatic relations with Peking in 1975, and they count on China to discourage Vietnam—which has become once again, as so often in its history, an expansionist power— from any chauvinist designs on Thailand.

In almost every way, people of Chinese descent have been far luckier in Thailand than those in the Muslim countries to the south, such as Malaysia

Scowling Chinese warriors equipped with swords, staves and javelins keep evil spirits away from Wat Po.

Sentinels of Stone

When King Rama I began building Wat Po and Wat Sutat in the late 18th Century, he acknowledged his ancestry by furnishing them with Chinese art objects, including some oddly matched stone guardians. Chinese warriors (above) bore the brunt of guard duty, but images of European soldiers (overleaf) gave potent back-up. Both sorts of statuary originally came to Thailand as ballast on royal rice boats returning from trade with China.

Statues of European soldiers in Wat Sutat's grounds wear the bemused smiles Chinese sculptors noticed among the first Westerners to visit the Orient.

and Indonesia, where religious differences have hindered integration and virtually precluded intermarriage. The Thais are naturally tolerant, and now that they are more closely involved in commerce themselves, rancour has died down. Discriminatory laws are less burdensome, because there are far fewer non-nationals for them to apply to. After 30 years of controlled immigration—even more tightly restricted since 1977 to a maximum of 100 persons of each nationality a year—an ever-increasing proportion of the Chinese community are locally born Thai subjects.

For their part, the Thai Chinese fully reciprocate the wise restraint with which they have, on the whole, been treated. Many of them readily opt for a Thai lifestyle, encouraging their children to qualify for good Thai schools and universities and adopting Thai names. The children of mixed marriages tend to practise Buddhism in its local form; Thai by education, they find it easier to take part in temple activities in which the Thai language is used. Like most Thai males, many of the men become monks for a time.

Most of the smaller ethnic communities that grew up in Bangkok during the heyday of rapid expansion have either declined in numbers or have been absorbed by marriage to an even greater extent than the Chinese. As a result they, too, are no longer distinguishable from the Thais. But one or two minorities have continued to be strikingly apart. Occasionally one comes across Thai nationals with a Malay or even Arab cast of features, sometimes made more noticeable by their dress on Friday, the Muslim Sabbath, when both sexes are attired in sarongs, and the men wear white skull-caps, the women a light cloth head-covering. They are followers of Islam, but in Bangkok are always known as "Thai Isalam". Most of them come from Thailand's southern peninsula region and, in common with the inhabitants of that area, they are predominantly ethnic Malay with an admixture of Thai blood. A few are descendants of merchants who came from Persia and from various parts of the Arab world more than two centuries ago to trade in the old capital of Ayutthaya. There are now about three million Thai Isalam in Thailand as a whole, and perhaps as many as 200,000 in Bangkok.

Mosques are found in most parts of the city, and a higher-than-average number of Thai Isalam live in their vicinity, though not in sufficient densities to create Muslim neighbourhoods. The older mosques are generally small, unpretentious wooden buildings, but some newer ones, more solidly built and splendid-looking, have arisen in the Hua Mark area in the north-east section of the city. Otherwise, the only obvious signs of the Thai Isalam are a few restaurants and cook-shops that sell dishes rather similar to those of south India. An unexpectedly large number of Muslim food-stalls may also be seen at Buddhist temple fairs—an instance of one religious community taking commercial advantage of another's festivities. In fact, so many Thai Isalam vendors of *khao muk gai*—the popular Muslim

dish of chicken with saffron rice—suddenly appear at these fairs that one must assume they carry on the trade as an occasional occupation only: when the fair is over, they return to other businesses.

There have been complaints among Malay Thais in the south of the country that insufficient attention has been paid to the needs of Muslim citizens; but in Bangkok any sense of difference or apartness would seem to be of their own choosing. They have their own hospitals and social insurance agencies, not because they would be unwelcome elsewhere but because they retain a strong sense of community and because Muslim philanthropists naturally prefer to spend money on their own people. Otherwise, of those Thai Isalam personally known to me, all are thoroughly integrated with the city's way of life—except of course in religious matters.

Another group of immigrants who still remain distinct are the settlers from the Indian subcontinent, many of them now Thai nationals. Indian families have lived in the city for generations, specializing as cloth merchants, jewellers and night-watchmen, and they remain alien only to the extent that they are so notably different in appearance—for they rarely intermarry with Thais. In restaurants one occasionally encounters parties of young Sikhs—tall, aquiline, long-haired and turbanned—chattering away in faultless Thai. They would be at a loss, presumably, if they were expected to converse in Punjabi. I have met Sikh boys who are as proud of being Thais as any other teenagers in Bangkok, yet their features and incipient beards are so strikingly alien that it is difficult to think of them as local people. (The Thais, as it happens, have a positive aversion to beards,

On display at a Chinese temple, realistic models constructed of paper and cardboard duplicate the worldly goods of a deceased Chinese businessman. Such models are burnt on the evening of a burial (right) so that the dead may continue to enjoy possessions in the afterlife.

perhaps because very few of them are capable of growing impressive ones; like other South-East Asian people, they are a smooth-skinned race.)

A third noticeable group in Bangkok are the so-called Thai Lao or Thai Isarn. The name Lao, also given to citizens of the neighbouring Republic of Laos, is applied in Thailand to nationals of the north-eastern provinces, the driest and most infertile part of the country. Isarn is the Thai dialect spoken by the people of that region. Properly speaking, the Thai Lao have grounds for claiming to be more Thai than the citizens of Bangkok and other people native to the Chao Phya delta, since very little racial mixing has taken place in the north-east. Yet, because the Thai Lao are generally poorly educated, they are sometimes the butt of disparaging remarks made by the people of Bangkok. Mostly they come to the capital as seasonal visitors, working as unskilled labourers after the rice harvest around New Year and returning home for the sowing of the new crop in August. One boast they can make is that they have left their culinary mark on the capital: in Bangkok's Isarn restaurants one can enjoy delicious garlic-impregnated fried chicken or such novelties as *laap*: highly spiced minced beef that is often eaten raw and causes fiery agonies to those un-accustomed to very hot chilies. Another delicacy is the meat of large, juicy lizards. In some of the Isarn cook-shops you can see dried or stuffed examples of these lizards hung around the walls of the dining-room as advertisements for the fresh ones.

Of course, none of these minority groups can compare with the Chinese in their contribution to the everyday life of Bangkok. Looking beyond shared clothes and similar features, one soon discovers how deeply the city has been influenced by the Chinese, and here and there one comes upon sights and sounds evocative of China long ago.

Although the Chinese nowadays live in all parts of Bangkok, they still predominate in the old commercial district of Sampeng, south-east of the Grand Palace.. Here, along the main arteries of Yaowaraj Road or Sampeng Lane or the narrow, tributary lanes, you can find a variety of shops where traditional crafts are plied. I particularly like the craft of lantern-making. Oiled paper is stretched on spherical rattan frames and then inscribed with large Chinese characters. On funeral lanterns that will be suspended over the doorways of bereaved families the characters appear in blue; they give the family name and sometimes the age of the deceased. But on lanterns for such auspicious occasions as weddings or the Chinese New Year the lettering is always in red. A favourite inscription is *Wan I Ju Shih*—"May everything turn out as one would wish"—while "Peace and harmony" is also very common. However, the lanterns with red lettering are nowadays rarely hung except as decorations in restaurants.

Some shops specialize in Chinese ritual objects, such as candles of deep-red wax, mirrors painted with magical devices to scare away demons from doorways, or small wooden shrines painted scarlet, shaped like temples and equipped with characters representing the deities who preside over commerce. These shrines can be seen installed in many shops and restaurants to bring the owners good fortune. Other ritual objects include coloured paper models of mansions, furniture, servants, cars,

On the floor of a cramped workshop, three children paint pieces for Chinese shrines that will join the completed wares cramming the shelves around them. A name painted on the front of each shrine indicates its dedication to a particular folk deity, such as the God of the Earth or the God of the Sky.

sewing-machines and even aeroplanes, which will be burnt during funeral rites, to be wafted up to heaven and so provide a deceased parent or spouse with every necessity for starting a new, comfortable life. Shops of this kind are usually fragrant with the scent of Chinese incense, which is more subtle and less cloying than the Indian or Thai varieties.

I also enjoy the pungent odour of herbs in old-style Chinese medicine shops. Here, in addition to many kinds of herbal remedies, can be found such exotic pick-me-ups as ginseng root, powdered deer's horn and even powdered "dragon bones" (fossils from the Gobi desert, perhaps?), all esteemed both as aphrodisiacs and for promoting longevity. As an excuse for dropping in at one of these shops, I often buy an ounce or two of dried chrysanthemum petals which, used like tea-leaves and with sugar added, make a soothing remedy for a cough or sore throat. If required, the medicine shop owners will direct one to an acupuncturist, or to an old-style Chinese physician able to distinguish six different pulses in each wrist. He may diagnose a complaint as being due to a lack of harmony within the body and then prescribe some dreadfully bitter herbal concoction.

Most of the narrow lanes in the Sampeng district run straight; and yet, because so many of them look alike, it is easy to lose one's way or fail to rediscover a remembered stall. Recently, I was searching for a little shop I had visited before. It sold Chinese musical instruments, including the two-stringed Mongolian fiddle, the so-called moon guitar (noted for its soft twang), various types of flute and clarinet, and drums, gongs and cymbals. I thought I recalled exactly where it was, but I never found it again.

Perhaps it is best to wander about this quarter without any specific objective, ready to welcome anything of interest. Once I came upon three very old women who, rather surprisingly, were dressed in the formal stiff white jackets and voluminous black silk trousers that were typical of China's southern coastal region many years ago. Behind them walked two little girls with bobbed hair, their cheeks and lips rouged as for a festival; they were carrying a huge ornamental basket specially made to transport layer upon layer of ceremonial cakes of the kind often exchanged between the families of newly engaged couples.

Out of curiosity I followed this little party unobtrusively. Soon we came to a Chinese temple where a fête in honour of the goddess Niang-Niang was taking place. Candles blazed on the altar and clouds of fragrant smoke arose from an incense tripod. In front of the altar was a long table piled high with beautifully arranged offerings of fruit and coloured cakes. A continual stream of worshippers made their way towards one end of the table where, after bowing three times, they picked up bamboo cylinders filled with numbered slivers of wood. These slivers were keys to their fortunes. Each person shook their cylinder so that just one sliver fell to the floor. The sliver was then exchanged for a paper bearing the same number and inscribed with an oracular prediction written in verse, together with an

Under the glare of a painted god (right), a woman seeks to ensure good fortune by purchasing a charm from a lay member of one of Bangkok's Chinese temples.

explanation in simple prose. When the first of the old women I had followed read her oracular verse, a smile of rapture transfigured her wrinkled face, revealing traces of a long-vanished beauty. But her companions received much less satisfying omens, and it was touching to see how hard she struggled to suppress her own delight out of sympathy for their disappointment. That was all—yet it was a rewarding outcome of a walk undertaken at random.

On another such walk I came upon a man with a huge, highly polished brass urn from which he dispensed a green liquid by the glassful in return for a small coin. Was it wine, medicine, a refreshment? It turned out to be a drink for cooling the blood—just what is needed around midday in the tropics—and it had an unusual, bitter-sweet taste that was quite new to me. The fun lay in sampling something altogether novel that may well have had a thousand-year-old history in China.

Outside the Sampeng district, the Chinese make their most noticeable contributions by running the city's shops and lending variety to its cuisine. The Chinese devotion to work is reflected in the long hours during which many of the shops stay open: from 8 or 9 o'clock in the morning to around 9 o'clock in the evening. These hours are maintained seven days a week throughout the year, except for a few days off at Chinese New Year. Now that the Thais engage in commerce more extensively, the Chinese year-end holiday no longer comes close to paralysing the city—as it used to do when grocers, food-stalls in the municipal markets and the various wholesale warehouses were almost entirely in Chinese hands. But householders still tend to stock up beforehand as if for a siege.

The Chinese are similarly predominant in the restaurant trade. When I first came to the city 30 years ago, Chinese restaurants used to reflect their customers' belief that the value of their money was found in the quality of the food, and not in frivolous decoration. This is still true of many plain little establishments, but the larger ones have changed enormously. Today, one eats sucking pig, shark's fins or Peking duck in palatial, ostentatiously Chinese surroundings. Off the main dining-hall there will be luxurious air-conditioned private rooms with special waiters. These inner rooms are equipped with one or two big round tables designed for parties of 10—an ideal number, since variety is the essence of a Chinese meal, and for groups of that size at least eight different dishes can be served. The dishes are placed in the centre of the table, where the diners can easily sample them all.

The private rooms are a blessing, for in the main hall there is likely to be a stage on which sexily posturing singers, accompanied by half a dozen energetic musicians, blare a repertoire of popular songs into amplifiers turned up to full volume. Here, one is obliged to point to the menu when ordering and table-talk becomes impossible.

For customers of more slender appetite or means, there are thousands of small Chinese cook-shops scattered throughout the city. They sell bowls of noodles with meat or shrimps, and plates of rice topped with slices of chicken and a spicy sauce. These dishes may cost as little as three *baht* (15 cents). In the smaller streets, portable Chinese restaurants are carried from place to place in search of business; they consist of a charcoal stove, a supply of fresh charcoal, dishes, bowls and chopsticks, and a cupboard containing half a dozen kinds of food. All these items may be attached to a special frame built on a tricycle, or else suspended from a bamboo carrying-pole with the stove dangling from one end, the food cupboard and utensils from the other and the itinerant cook in the middle. The dishes these cooks provide at a moment's notice are often extremely tasty. My own favourite is a snack locally called *sarapao*, consisting of hot steamed buns with a stuffing of roast pork or of boiled eggs and pieces of chicken. One has to admire the men who convey these great loads in the hot sun, often covering several miles a day yet with tempers so un-impaired that they are always ready to joke with customers while the food is being cooked. Hygiene, admittedly, is rudimentary: the single basin of water in which the dishes and bowls are washed has to do duty a great many times in one day; but few of Bangkok's citizens are deterred by this thought, and harmful effects seem rare.

Among other Chinese pedlars are those who sell a modern delicacy by which I confess I have never been tempted: a dollop of ice cream served on a hunk of bread with a topping of condensed milk. Then there are the sellers of freshly sliced fruits—hard, unripe mangoes and guavas are among the most popular—which are dipped in a powder compounded of salt, sugar and chili.

The survival of so many of these little enterprises is everyday proof that not all the descendants of Chinese immigrants have become millionaires or even moderately successful businessmen. On the other hand, one rarely sees destitute Chinese. Most, with their appetite for hard work, are able to make more than a bare living, and those who fail are cared for by the various mutual-aid organizations of a more or less religious nature run by the Chinese community.

Nearly all the buildings in Bangkok that have retained a characteristic Chinese appearance, are—if not actually temples—temple-like buildings that house some mutual-aid body. For example, the so-called Halls of Virtue, normally connected with particular cults, offer refuge for elderly people (mostly women) in surroundings where they can prepare for the next life by meditation and pious rituals. The Halls of Virtue are also used as places of religious retreat for people of all ages who stay there for anything from a week to 10 days; during that time they eat strictly vegetarian food, both out of compassion for living creatures of all kinds and because this diet is thought most suitable for extensive meditation.

Two women sip herbal drinks concocted at a specialist shop in Bangkok's Chinese district of Sampeng. Brews made with herbs, bark or roots are drunk by the Chinese both as refreshment and to remedy such minor complaints as stomach upsets or headaches.

Other buildings of this kind include the headquarters of the so-called Clan Associations. Such associations bring together people who have a common surname or whose ancestors came from the same district of China. The members of an association have an obligation to help one another generously and to look after the indigent, thus not only doing good to others but also gaining merit for themselves. Each of these buildings contains a hall in which the clan members may hold weddings and other ceremonies, especially for honouring the dead. At the back of the hall stands an altar, and on the wall behind it are ranged tier upon tier of spirit-tablets—rectangles of wood decorated with carving and gold and red or gold and green lacquer. These tablets are inscribed in fine calligraphy with the names of the departed and are believed to provide the spirits with some kind of corporeal home. Whenever a clan member dies, the association gathers to perform the sacred rites that will save the dead person's spirit from wandering homeless in the underworld. In their fear of such a fate, some clansmen have spirit-tablets placed in the hall during their lifetimes, so that they can occasionally inspect them and be confident that all is prepared. In such cases, the name will be covered with a drape until the moment when the spirit departs.

The sharing of a common surname does not necessarily imply consanguinity, since the 900 million Chinese in the world share less than 200 surnames; but it does imply an honorary kinship, and this bond is often very strong. I once asked a Chinese friend with the exceedingly common surname Li whether his clan association was prepared, if necessary, to look after all the Lis in Bangkok.

"We have no rule that compels us to do that," he replied. "Normally the Li Association cares only for the poor and needy among its own members. Still, I believe our attachment to the surname handed down by our ancestors is so strong that even if a Korean or Vietnamese Li—they have Lis too, you know—were to turn up at our Ancestral Hall and claim urgent assistance, we should find it impossible to refuse him. Even in their cases, there is a remote possibility that we descend from the same original clan. How could we face our ancestors in the next world if they had grounds for charging us with the neglect of one of their progeny?"

"Do you really believe you will come face to face with your first ancestors in the next world?" I asked.

He thought for a while before answering: "I think not, but I also think it is very good for us morally to act as though we were sure of meeting them. And then, how can we be sure of *not* meeting them? I dare say the idea that our ancestors are watching us critically has its origins in the same impulse that makes Christians believe in an all-knowing God. Something is watching us, even if it is nothing more than our own consciences. It is good to be aware of that Something and so behave a little less like bandits and hooligans than we humans are apt to do."

Other associations very similar to the Clan Associations, but open to all who care to belong, are the Benevolent Societies. They collect dues from wealthy members and prosperous firms and apply them to good works. A part is set aside for members' funeral rites, but the bulk is devoted to running public clinics, dispensaries and maternity homes where the poor receive free treatment and other patients pay according to their means. These, and a variety of other welfare services, are a valuable supplement to those provided—often inadequately—by the government. Although the donors are almost always of Chinese descent, recipients may be of any race, since the purpose is to make merit by helping all in need.

In Bangkok, as elsewhere, some Chinese mutual-aid organizations that were originally formed with admirable motives have developed into secret societies operating in the underworld of gambling, drugs, prostitution and protection rackets. Often they wage internecine feuds. True, these societies have not shown signs of affiliation with the Triads, ruthless gangs that originated as secret patriot groups in 17th-Century China and now control organized crime in Hong Kong and elsewhere in the Far East. No doubt the secret societies have lacked incentive in Bangkok, where even after the Second World War gambling and opium dens were legal. However, since the early 1970s, when stringent penalties were introduced for drug peddling, and gambling controls were tightened, the opportunity for racketeering has increased. Local drug rings are now known to have powerful international connections, since Bangkok lies on one of the main smuggling routes from the notorious Golden Triangle, a mountainous region at the meeting point of Burma, Thailand and Laos that is the source of much of the world's opium and heroin.

Aesthetically, the Chinese influence in Bangkok has been uneven. It was not to be expected that the illiterate immigrants of a century ago would bring with them all the highly refined aspects of their culture, or reproduce the patina of an art built up over millennia. They were good at carpentry, furniture-making and ceramic decoration, but could hardly aspire to high achievements in poetry, classical opera, jade carving or delicate scroll painting. As for their architecture in Bangkok, it is a tribute to good intentions, at best. Their temples, some Buddhist, others dedicated to folk deities, are sometimes moderately impressive. Mostly small, they are tucked away down narrow lanes, and the oldest are authentic examples of southern Chinese architecture, with elaborately curling roofs surmounted by mythical monsters. The newer temples are built entirely of concrete and though attempts have been made to reproduce in this unpromising material the ancient structure of elaborately painted beams resting on huge lacquered pillars of wood, the effects have not always been happy.

The largest of these concrete temples, Wat Poman, is a Buddhist place of worship, very spacious and ornate, yet incongruously standing in an

Chinese Buddhist monks in distinctive trousered garb stride across the courtyard of Wat Poman, a garish, all-concrete temple completed in 1969. Many of Bangkok's Chinese practise a form of Buddhism that emphasizes the attainment of salvation through worship of the supernatural rather than through the accumulation of personal merit. Some of the Chinese temples in the city have no Buddhist associations at all; instead they are dedicated to folk gods who are honoured through prayers, offerings of food or goods, and the burning of candles, incense and paper money.

obscure lane in a half-developed area close to the southernmost bulge of the river. No doubt the temple was located here because the land needed for so large a project was suitably inexpensive at the time of purchase. Completed in 1969 and vaunted by its abbot as "the equal in splendour of the Forbidden City of Peking", the temple is to my mind a gigantic chamber of horrors.

The exterior does have some merits, notably a breath-taking set of roofs that recall the fantastic palaces of Taoist immortals one sees rising above the clouds in old Chinese paintings. In the forecourt is a unique collection of pagoda-like structures in the Chinese, Tibetan and Nepalese styles, also built of concrete but very attractive in their way. This promising first impression serves only to increase the shock, or indeed series of shocks, that the visitor meets within. One passes from hall to hall, courtyard to courtyard, each with garishly tiled floors and brilliantly painted concrete walls, ceilings and beams—a riot of clashing colours, with gaudy reds, livid blues, bilious greens and jaundiced yellows all fighting for the honour of being most outrageous. Possibly these colours would not deserve such unkind adjectives if they could be viewed individually; it is the effect of placing them together that is so harsh. Visitors are escorted through the temple by young novices, and to hear them complacently repeating, in their vast ignorance, their abbot's boastful comparison with the exquisitely beautiful palaces of the Manchu emperors is like being forced to listen to some atrocious blasphemy. As for the holy images within the temple, some are the work of a very indifferent Italian sculptor who has succeeded in making the Buddha look like a Renaissance ne'er-do-well in borrowed clothes.

Aesthetically happier are the traditional Chinese operas. Although theatres presenting them have (like those offering traditional Thai dance and opera) largely succumbed to the competition of cinemas and television, troupes of strolling Chinese players still give open-air performances. Dressed in richly embroidered robes, their faces made up to resemble multicoloured masks, they strut on temporary stages erected in temples and market-places. The stages creak, groan and threaten to collapse beneath the violent, marvellously acrobatic movements of embattled warriors re-enacting the wars of a thousand years ago. Lovelorn maidens and the faithful wives of men conscripted to fight in the Mongolian wastes—or to construct the Great Wall of China—wail their sorrows into microphones; and venal magistrates still respond to the pleas of their kneeling victims with spine-chilling laughter, transporting one back through the centuries to the heyday of imperial China.

Pervading every aspect of Chinese daily life is the vast host of gods, spirits and demons they have added to Bangkok's already teeming pantheon. The Chinese venerate more gods and spirits than any other people in the world, Hindus possibly excepted; paradoxically, I have found few who believe strongly in any one deity. Yet behind this duality of too much belief and no belief at all lies a vague but very strong moral sense of what it is fitting for human beings to do.

The immense capacity of the Chinese for hard work, even in Bangkok's enervating climate, no doubt has much to do with the grim lessons their ancestors learnt during long years of penury in the Swatow area. But the fact that this capacity has hardly been impaired after decades of relatively soft living in Bangkok makes one suspect a deeper cause. I think it may lie in their concept of the universe, not exactly as the work of a divine creator, but as a creation governed by inflexible moral law, from which man departs at his peril. Their notion of what is or is not morally right—depending as it does on rigid loyalty to elders, family and clan—may differ fundamentally from that of the Thais, with their flexible interpretation of Buddhist precepts. But whatever it may be, it seems the key to their success in a foreign environment.

Whether intermarriage between the Chinese and the Thais has brought benefits to the local population, as King Mongkut hoped, is an open question. There is a widespread belief in Bangkok that the children of such mixed marriages do have an advantage over those of pure Thai stock. What is certain is that if the Chinese had not supplied their productive skills and their qualities of industry and enterprise at a time when such talents were lacking, Bangkok would have been a very different place. As rulers and administrators, the Thai majority have moulded the city's development and sometimes they have regarded the Chinese way of life as incompatible with their own. That they no longer do so is evidence that a long relationship between two peoples has culminated in a happy marriage.

The Silk-Maker's Art

Silhouetted against a window in a workshop in east Bangkok, a skilled spinner concentrates as he attaches the delicate silk warp to the cylinder of a loom.

One of Bangkok's most buoyant industries—the making of silk cloth—is also one of its oldest. The art was brought out of China by the Thais when they emigrated from there nine centuries ago, and it is still practised today with hand looms in hundreds of homes and backstreet workshops. Because Thailand's silk larvae spin unusually soft, thick fibres, the local fabric accepts dyes more readily than silk made elsewhere.

The craft declined in the 19th Century when Western traders flooded the country with cheap cotton. But after the Second World War an American businessman named Jim Thompson, who had travelled through the country as an intelligence officer, launched a silk-exporting firm that revitalized the craft almost overnight. Bangkok's producers now make about three million yards of the fabric for Western markets each year.

In the steamy atmosphere of a small factory's dyeing room, youthful workers wear only shorts, sandals and gloves as they colour skeins of silk in heated vats.

In the yard of her klong-side home in the Baan Krua district, a woman uses a bicycle wheel to wind silk thread while her neighbour hangs newly dyed skeins to dry.

Operating a fast flying shuttle loom in a home in the Thung Mahamek district of the city, a weaver works on a brocade fabric that will be 260 yards long.

Preparing a screen used to impart an arabesque pattern to a fabric, an employee in a silk-printing factory dips her brush in varnish that blocks dye where desired.

Factory workers carefully align their silk screen over the pattern as they move down a length of undyed silk and add areas of colour to an exotic jungle scene.

6

A Talent for Pleasure

Important characteristics of a community are sometimes revealed by the frequency of certain words in the local language. In Bangkok, words forever on people's lips are *sanuk*, meaning "enjoyable" or "good fun", and *sabai*, meaning "comfortable" in the sense of feeling deliciously cool, at ease, pleasantly replete. Used together, they express the acme of well-being. The concomitants of this state need not be elaborate; it is *sanuk* just to be with a lot of happy people; it is *sabai* to snooze on a rainy afternoon or enjoy a refreshing evening breeze.

Thais often use the words when a foreigner would least expect them. One evening I drove with a party of Thai friends to a stretch of the Chao Phya River where we hoped to get a good view of the Festival of Floating Lights, held every November on a night when the moon is full. Miniature floats containing lit candles are set adrift to honour the river spirits, and they make a very pretty spectacle on the rippling water. But on this occasion there was such a rush of cars and spectators that we were unable to get near the river bank, let alone glimpse the dancing points of flame we had specially come to see. I was about to suggest a change of venue when, glancing at my friends, I noticed that their eyes were shining with pleasure. "*Sanuk, sanuk,*" they murmured.

"I should call it a miserable fiasco!"

"No, no. You don't often see such a lovely crush of people as this. And the breeze off the water! *Sabai!*"

Another clue to the Bangkok temperament is the answer most often given if you meet an acquaintance by chance and ask where he is going. "*Pai teeo,*" comes the smiling response: "Just wandering around for fun". This phrase signifies anything from window-shopping to having a jolly evening with wine, women and song—or just with a woman (no wine or song). It includes practically any activity, in fact, other than work or a cremation, for people in Bangkok take most things in life as fun.

The most positively *sanuk* activities include eating, drinking, sex, sports, going to a temple to make merit, and attending fairs and festivals where one can be sure of being part of a large, pleasure-bent crowd. The order of importance will naturally depend on individual taste, but eating is certain to rank high. It is not that people in Bangkok have gross appetites. On the contrary, they are inclined to eat sparingly at meals, picking at various small dishes and seldom helping themselves to more than a couple of heaped tablespoonfuls of rice, if that much. But in between meals, they are dedicated munchers. In and out of office

Under tinted lights, a go-go girl writhes provocatively in one of the several hundred nightclubs that flourish in Bangkok. Many such establishments also employ "hostesses", who chat with clients and serve as dancing partners.

buildings, government departments or even police stations—and all along railway platforms—relays of teenage vendors dart about with trays of iced coffee or hot snacks. Nor is that all, for people generally bring to work or school a few light refreshments—translucent slivers of dried and sweetened beef, perhaps; crunchy wafers of glazed banana, or crisp, tubular biscuits that melt almost to nothing on the tongue. After work, some will visit stalls selling "evening sweets", with ingredients that might become rancid if the food were displayed during the hottest hours of the day.

An ingredient essential to many sweets is coconut cream, not to be confused with ordinary coconut milk. It is a white, fatty liquid made from the tender white flesh of young coconuts, grated in water and squeezed through a straining cloth. Mixed with egg and sugar, coconut cream makes a rich custard. Young pumpkins are often stuffed with it and then steamed until their flesh becomes as tender as the filling itself. Another popular sweet, made (like so many Thai foods) to tempt both eye and palate, looks like a jam-filled blancmange, but is actually coconut flesh, powdered, glutinous rice and coconut cream mixed with a little sugar. The "jam filling" is often made from crushed beans and palm sugar. Each mouthful is contained in a tiny, open-topped box skilfully fashioned from the fragrant leaves of a *toei* shrub (a type of screw pine); when the box is pressed, the sweet pops into the mouth.

Besides sweets proper to certain times of day, there are sweets eaten at certain seasons. A few tradition-minded families still send to the country for rice that is specially harvested when the grains are only just beginning to

Reaching across an enticing array of foods, a vendor assists a customer at a sidewalk stall. The wide choice of inexpensive foods available in the streets of Bangkok includes door-to-door delivery of hot soup at 1 baht (5 cents) a bowl.

More than a hundred dried squid are neatly ranged according to size on a cycle-driven cart in Lumpini Park. Customers have them grilled on the spot, and the squid are then wrapped in bags made out of old magazine pages.

form. From these tender, green rice grains, boiled in the husk with sugar and *toei* leaves, comes a pale green, creamy liquid much esteemed for its delicate fragrance. It is eaten from little leaf boxes in the same way as the blancmange sweet. A less extravagant seasonal sweet—so substantial that it makes a lunch in itself, and so delicious that one can eat it day after day—consists of freshly sliced *ok rong* mangoes (a species with pale yellow flesh and greenish skin) served with sweetened, glutinous rice and coconut cream. Mangoes ripen in April and May, but if they grew throughout the year, I should never want to have any other kind of lunch.

However, there are plenty of alternatives. With the appearance not long ago of a Lebanese restaurant in Bangkok, it can be said that no major cuisine of Asia, Europe or the Americas is unrepresented in the city. Moreover, there are hotels that regularly hold international food festivals, with fare flown in from the countries featured. Of course, none of these places can be considered typical of Bangkok, in that they are not patronized by the mass of its citizens. Even the Thai-style restaurants found in some of the international hotels are quite unauthentic. Here, one is served with courses artistically set out in elaborately decorated dishes and lidded bowls like those to be found in old, aristocratic Thai homes; the pretty serving-girls are dressed in sleek versions of traditional Thai costume, and the whole setting is meant to evoke an atmosphere of Old Siam. Unfortunately, the Thai recipes in these establishments are deprived of chili, garlic and spices to suit the presumed tastes of Western and Japanese visitors, and the results are as insipid as boiled turnip. As a Thai friend of mine once declared of such restaurants, "They remind me of those expensive places in Japan that seem to cater to a race whose tastebuds are located in the eye!"

The popular places to eat in Bangkok are the ubiquitous Chinese restaurants and cook-shops, the Isarn restaurants with their lizard specialities from north and north-east Thailand, and the growing number of places run by Bangkok Thais and serving Bangkok-style food. The restaurants most favoured by well-to-do customers are set in gardens, although nowadays land is so costly that for every tree—hung with coloured electric bulbs—there may be 20 close-packed tables. More economical are the hundreds of small indoor places with nothing special about their décor. There are also a few floating restaurants—converted rice-barges—near Memorial Bridge on the Thonburi bank of the river. Here, though the appointments are starkly simple, one eats much better than on the luxurious motor-barges where tourists dine while being carried a short distance up and down the river. The Thais are generally indifferent to where they eat so long as they eat well.

Among the eating places most frequented by those with slender budgets (and not fussy about hygiene) are the large, roofed-in, municipal markets where—in addition to stalls selling foodstuffs and general merchandise—there are many scores of stalls, each with a few chairs and tables, that specialize in one or two particular dishes. One can either enjoy a peripatetic meal by sitting down at a different table for each course, or remain at one table and have extra dishes brought over from neighbouring stalls. Every evening, these markets are packed by convivial diners with whom it is easy to strike up a casual acquaintance.

Bangkok-style Thai dishes are typically prepared with a liberal use of basil, coriander, mint, shallots, ginger, pepper, garlic, spring onions, the inevitable chilies and the ubiquitous fish sauce, *nam pla*, (which is actually an exudation of sun-dried shrimps kneaded with salt). Thai cooks make use of almost all available materials: fish, prawns, crab and mussels; pork, beef, chicken and duck; and many kinds of vegetable. Among favourite seafoods are fried shrimp-paste balls, crabmeat minced with pork and served in the shell, and boiled or fried squid, enjoyed for its tough texture. Meats fried with garlic and pepper, or with basil leaf, are popular; alternatively, they are often served raw for roasting over a miniature charcoal grill set on the table. Among vegetables, a thin but tasty locally grown asparagus, and a miniature sweetcorn (each cob is no bigger than a thimble) are particularly good.

After these courses may come *tom yam*, a highly spiced soup often made with shrimp, fish or chicken. Though it is truly delicious, the uninitiated should beware of something green that may lurk beneath innocent fragments of coriander leaf—namely, tiny chilies known, on account of their shape and size, as "rats' excreta". Biting into one of them

In an unpretentious Bangkok seafood restaurant, Thais settle down to an evening meal of rice and half a dozen bowls of fish specialities, vegetables and soup.

releases a fiery oil that can smear the tongue and lips most painfully. Even some Thais avoid them, though others chew them happily.

Most meals will end with fruit. Among Bangkok's prodigious variety of tropical species, there is one—the durian—to which nobody can remain indifferent, so violently does it demand to be either loved or abhorred. By its foes, the durian is said to stink worse than a long-clogged drain, and most airlines or ships will not allow a durian to be carried aboard. It resembles a rugger ball, but is sharply spiked as though intended for use in some diabolical game, and its rind is so hard that it cannot be opened by anything less than a kitchen chopper. Yet its addicts—and these include nine-tenths of the city's population—say that it is perfumed like *amrita*, the nectar of the Hindu gods. My first taste of a durian sent me retching from the table; but the encomiums heaped upon it convinced me that I was missing out on one of life's great experiences, so I persevered when the next durian season came round, suppressing my nausea until, with the suddenness of a revivalist conversion, disgust gave place to ecstasy. Now I seldom pass a durian stall without taking deep, appreciative breaths; yet the pleasure of its fragrance pales beside that of sucking the delicate white flesh from the pale yellow stones to which it clings.

For a people so devoted to *sanuk* in all its forms, the Thais have been surprisingly uninventive in the matter of drink. Thai men (though seldom Thai women) love drinking, but traditional local beverages are limited to palm toddy—a heady liquid like strong, creamy beer—and various kinds of rice spirit, none of them especially enjoyable for their flavour. Some decades ago, to compensate for this lack of variety, a Scottish whisky distiller was invited to Bangkok to see what could be made locally in the way of a palatable drink to go with soda. This canny Scot is remembered (or perhaps forgotten) as the creator of what is now the national beverage —*Mekong*. It is distilled from rice but is smoother and more pleasant in odour than most rice spirits. Though nothing like whisky, it is very good. Next, German brewers were invited to try their hand, and there are now two locally produced lagers good enough to make imports from Europe unnecessary. Unfortunately, wine-making, which began a few years ago with locally grown grapes, has not had the same success. Thai wines— both red and white—are not only over sweet, but lack flavour and alcoholic content.

Among non-alcoholic drinks, iced coffee, brewed from locally grown beans, has largely displaced China tea, though some Chinese shop-keepers still keep utensils handy for making tea in the manner introduced from Swatow a century ago. Good quality semi-green (that is, partially fermented) tea-leaves are used to concoct an infusion so strong that it is normally drunk from porcelain cups no bigger than liqueur glasses. The tea is not esteemed as a remedy for thirst, nor even for its flavour—the little cup is drained at a gulp—but for its delicious after-taste.

Crouching on a scaffold platform, a workman steadies a section of a giant poster that is being assembled to advertise a forthcoming Thai film. Five major film studios in Bangkok together turn out several hundred films each year for an enthusiastic public. Thai movie-goers like their films long: many run for three hours or more.

For all those votaries of *sanuk* who put sex before food and drink—or after, it makes no matter—Bangkok is a good place to be. Living up to its reputation as the Paris of the East, it has an enormous variety of extremely *sanuk* sexual establishments—nightclubs, massage parlours, bunny clubs, and other girlie haunts. A visitor will have no difficulty locating these places: most taxi drivers carry cards listing, in a variety of languages, the whereabouts of night-spots that cater to every taste. Massage parlours are found in most shopping streets, and the main centres for bars and night-clubs are Silom, Patpong and Suriwong roads in the south of the city and Sukhumvit Road and adjacent areas in the east.

People sensitive to Bangkok's public image tend to blame the hyper-development of night-life on the city's role as a rest-and-recreation centre for the American military during the Vietnam War. There is no denying that the half-million G.I.s who visited Bangkok during the 1960s brought about a mushrooming of night-spots—nor that the growing volume of tourism has helped maintain the impetus. But by no means all the city's night-time haunts were opened to accommodate G.I.s or tourists, and many are located in districts to which visitors seldom find their way. In truth, sexual entertainment is scarcely foreign to the spirit of Bangkok, although for the most part it continues within the limits set by the traditional Thai concern for public restraint and modesty.

Streets such as Patpong are lined with girlie bars where the patrons buy the company of pretty hostesses at so much for half an hour plus the price of treating the girl to a glass or two of cola masquerading as whisky. Plenty of drinking and cheerful chatter takes place against a background of soft music and dim lights, but nothing that occurs on the premises could be deemed improper. Should a patron and hostess slip out and hail a taxi, that is their privilege as free individuals. The same sort of restraint prevails in disco bars, where patrons may dance with their own or hired partners. And in bars offering solo dance shows, where girl after girl leaps upon the stage to do her act, the dancers retain bikini-like costumes in order to keep the show within the law. If a part of the costume happens to slip down now and then, it is pretty certain that the patrons have been carefully surveyed and that no suspected plain-clothes policeman is among them.

Many bungalow-style motels in the city offer short-stay accommodation with maximum decorum. Beneath each of the bedrooms is a small curtained garage. As soon as a car has driven in, watchful attendants with carefully averted gaze run to draw the curtain so as to preserve the complete anonymity of visiting couples. Massage parlours are equally circumspect about their arrangements. On arrival, patrons find themselves before a large two-way mirror through which they can see, but not be seen. Behind it sit from 20 to well over 100 demurely clad girls, chatting to one another or leafing through the latest film magazines. Each has a number prominently displayed on her blouse so that the client can ask for the girl who catches

Eight-Armed Warriors

For many citizens and visitors, Bangkok's most exciting entertainment is Thai boxing, staged several nights a week at stadiums in the city. Derived from medieval martial arts, the sport is sometimes called "eight-armed fighting" because—in addition to pummelling an opponent with fists—each boxer makes devastating use of his bare feet for kicking, and his knees and elbows for jabbing.

Before the fight, the contestants pray for victory (above), thank their trainers, and salute the King. Then, to the accompaniment of pounding drums and wailing pipe music, they punch and kick in a hypnotic display of balletic grace and murderous ferocity. Matches last for five three-minute rounds and are won on points awarded by a referee and two judges—unless one boxer inflicts so much damage on his opponent that the referee has to stop the bout.

his fancy. To all appearances, these parlours are respectable places where a visitor can take a hot bath in the privacy of a cubicle, to be followed by an invigorating massage on a couch placed conveniently beside the bath-tub. Should anything less innocent transpire (which, judging by the popularity of these places, must often happen), that is a private matter to be arranged by those concerned.

The availability of so many pleasure girls in Bangkok—perhaps 200,000, no one really knows—is a result, first and foremost, of rural poverty. Most of the girls come from families owning insufficient land to support many grown-up children and have been forced to migrate to the city in search of employment of any kind; some, though, have gladly given up the back-breaking task of cultivating rice-paddies under a burning sun, hoping to make an easier living in prostitution. If successful, they may be able to earn more money than a top civil servant. But the Thai attitude towards sexual pleasures is also a strong influence. Though chastity is held to be spiritually exalting, laxity is regarded less as positively sinful than as unwise for those who cherish exalted goals, just as it would be unwise for a boxer to neglect his training. On the whole, Thai families expect women to be chaste, and strict chaperonage of daughters is still common; but the menfolk have traditionally been allowed a very large measure of freedom. Youths in their late teens, apart from some high-minded students and very serious Buddhists, look upon visits to brothels as a recreation enjoyable and necessary for health, but otherwise of no particular importance.

Pleasure girls do not have Bangkok night-life entirely to themselves. Sometimes mingling with the bar hostesses there are transvestites known as *gatoei*. So cleverly do they impersonate attractive young girls that it takes a sharp eye to spot them. Occasionally, though, *gatoei* are more noticeable. For a short while a few years ago, the Bangkok nights were enlivened by *gatoei* prostitutes, identifiable by their hoarse voices and uninhibited conduct, who defied the ban on street-walkers by cruising about in taxis and virtually snatching startled pedestrians from the sidewalks— a breach of public decorum that was soon halted by the police.

Gatoei have been tolerantly accepted as a distinct third sex in this part of South-East Asia for many centuries. Even before the establishment of the first Thai kingdom in the 13th Century, they were common in Cambodia, where effeminate boys performed as temple dancers. In the 9th Century, a Chinese envoy to Cambodia, then the suzerain power in this area, complained of the bold attempts made by transvestites to seduce his staff.

Even today, it is thought unreasonable to penalize *gatoei* for behaving according to their nature. Their exaggeratedly girlish gestures do cause laughter, but this they accept as well-merited applause. I was once present at a large garden party given by a Bangkok bus company at which, just for a change, the servants engaged to serve the food were all *gatoei*, a detail that nobody seemed to think especially odd. And I have seen dozens of *gatoei*, all carrying identical sunshades, marching as a unit in a civic procession in a northern city. In Bangkok these days males may be in trouble if they appear on the streets in female costume, but this has hardly inconvenienced the *gatoei* who, adopting the unisex garments fashionable among young people, pretend to be girls dressed as boys.

With their love of pleasure, their readiness to try new pastimes and their pride in being up to date, people in Bangkok have enthusiastically adopted modern sports. Athletics, swimming, water-skiing, judo, golf, tennis, soccer, rugby football and basketball are all popular. Largely as a consequence, most traditional sports have declined or gone out of fashion, but Thai boxing still draws large crowds at two stadiums in Bangkok where matches in various weight classes are put on several nights a week throughout the year. The programmes include a good deal of ritual, reflecting the sport's derivation from ancient martial arts. The boxers enter the ring wearing coloured cords around their heads, boxing-gloves but no shoes, and kneel to offer prayers to their teachers. Then, with a clash of gongs and cymbals and the notes of a harsh-sounding kind of flageolet, the fight begins. It is accompanied throughout by this music, and by shouts of advice, encouragement or contempt from the crowd. At first, the boxers seem to be dancing rather than fighting seriously; then suddenly one will flail out with his feet. Knees, too, and legs, elbows or shoulders are all used for striking; and crippling blows are delivered more often with the feet than with the gloves. The boxers, usually light-weight, depend on speed and agility rather than strength; thus, a contest becomes an exhibition of graceful movement—although in fact it can be every bit as bloody and dangerous as ordinary boxing.

A few other traditional sports retain a following. Kite-fighting, for example, can still be seen in the early evenings from February to June, when the wind blows strongly from the south. These sky battles, held at the Pramane Ground near the Grand Palace, are waged by two contestants. One flies the *chula*, a "male" kite that is star-shaped, measures five feet across and has a thick, barbed string; the other flies the *pak pao*, a "female" kite that is much smaller, with a thinner, unbarbed string, and a long tail that is used to ensnare the points of the star-shaped *chula*. The male kite can win by tangling or severing the string of its opponent; or the acrobatic female kite may seize the victory by dragging the *chula* to the ground. An audience of hundreds often watches these frays, usually with much excited betting on the outcome.

Young men at the universities occasionally play another venerable Thai game—*takraw*—in which a braided rattan ball may be knocked into the air with head, shoulders, elbows, knees, calves, ankles or feet, but never with the hands. The players' movements are beautiful to watch, especially when someone, catching the ball on the back of his heel (which requires that he

sense exactly where the ball will fall behind him), kicks it upwards over his head and back into the circle of play.

Occasionally, too, one sees displays of the old martial arts, including duels between men sometimes armed with two swords apiece. These contests look exceedingly dangerous, but well-trained swordsmen wield their weapons with such precision that each lightning blow is neatly countered before it can do any damage. To reduce the likelihood of an accident—which could cost a limb or even a life—the swordsmen agree to take turns attacking and defending, and they also set a time limit on the contest so they do not become dangerously tired.

The most dramatic of these sword-fights are held in arenas in the 20-acre amusement park of TIMland—an acronymic abbreviation of "Thailand In Miniature"—where tourists can view a range of traditional Thai arts, including village crafts, elephant logging, silk-weaving and lacquer-making. Less impressive sword-fights, aimed at the same sort of audience, are sometimes put on in hotels, restaurants or nightclubs, along with displays of Thai classical and folk dancing. The standard of swordsmanship or dancing in such places may not be very high, but at least the demand for artists is kept alive and the continuance of training facilities is assured. In this respect, tourism, in spite of the harm it does in raising prices and corrupting standards of integrity in a city, does help perpetuate what is truly picturesque.

To the Thai balletomane, the essence of refined *sanuk* is afforded only by a proper performance of *khon*, a highly formalized type of dance-drama that has developed over many centuries. Full-length performances are now presented only at the National Theatre, which is heavily subsidized by the government. Every *khon* ballet is based upon one of the episodes in the Thai epic, the *Ramakien*. A hundred or more dancers—wearing spangled and brocaded costumes, gold crowns and jewelled ornaments, and representing animals and supernatural beings as well as humans—enact a story sung by singers off-stage. The orchestral accompaniment includes the sweet music of xylophones, the chiming of a set of bell-like gongs set in a circular frame of scarlet and gold lacquer, the harsher wail of horns, and the crash of drums and cymbals.

In these dramas, the faces of the human characters are smoothed of all but the most delicate hints of expression; the animal and mythical characters—the demon hosts of the evil King of Ceylon, the monkey warriors led by the monkey god Hanuman, and the horses, deer and giant birds that figure in the plot—wear extravagant, vividly coloured masks depicting expressions ranging from simian playfulness to fiendish ferocity. As the gorgeously clad characters dance with stately footwork, the eye is riveted by the rhythmic, intricate play of hands, arms and torsos.

On witnessing a *khon* performance for the first time, the viewer may feel that the pace is too slow and the gestures too ritualistic. (The humorous

Make-up, a wig and a lavishly sequinned costume combine to disguise the young man (left) who is being dressed for a female role in a khon ballet: a classical form of dance-drama in which all parts are traditionally played by men. In the scene above, staged in a private garden by students at Thammasat University, the white-masked figure represents the monkey god Hanuman, a key character in the Hindu legends that provide plots for all khon ballets.

moments are the easiest to appreciate, particularly the way in which the monkey characters enrage the demons with their insulting posturings.) But presently it becomes clear that all these gestures form part of a great and difficult art. Much of the story, in fact, is told with movements of hand and finger, and there are said to be no less than 68 distinct finger gestures, each with its own evocative yet precise meaning. Thus, many years of arduous training must precede an actor's first appearance. Similar skills are needed in *lakhon,* a form of classical dancing that closely resembles *khon* in every way except for the cast. All the masculine roles are played by women—for *lakhon* was originally performed in the inner courts of the Grand Palace, where no males except the king were allowed.

Traditional Thai music, using instruments and techniques that originated in other Asian countries, has also declined in popularity, though not so disastrously as ballet. The forms that accompany performances of *khon* have affinities with the music of Burma and Indonesia. Over the centuries the Thais composed hundreds of tunes that were intended to underscore the actions and emotions of the dancers. For example, sorrow could be indicated by any of 21 melodies, anger had 13 melodic equivalents, and stage actions such as sitting, walking, greeting or conquering could all be expressed musically. Other types of Thai music betray Malaysian and Indian origins, and those employing flutes and two-stringed fiddles are reminiscent of Chinese court music.

Today, these ancient and subtle sounds have been all but drowned by Western-type music. All over the city, transistor radios blare out pop songs from early morning until late at night, varying this fare with a kind of music called *sakolor,* in which modern instruments accompany the singing of vaguely Thai melodies. In my opinion (shared by some Thai friends), *sakolor* songs are among the dreariest to be heard anywhere in the world. But the Bangkok public never seems to tire of them, and it is hard to find places in the city where one is safe from their assaults. As for popular dance, *ramwong* reigns supreme. This is a modified folk dance: couples join a large circle and perform simple, repetitious steps. There is almost no bodily contact; instead, the dancers hold their arms high and form random gestures with their fingers that are virtually impossible for Europeans to imitate successfully. *Ramwong* is enormously popular, and fulfils a social need by bringing couples together in an irreproachable way.

In one aspect of the city's life, tradition survives more or less intact and continues to provide *sanuk* activities for the mass of people: the traditional festivals, many religious in nature, are celebrated during the course of the year with much of the old vigour. The festival of Songkran (marking the old Thai New Year in mid-April) has always been an occasion for great hilarity. Until a few years ago it provided an opportunity for youths to drench pedestrians and motorists with water.

With expressions ranging from wonder to hilarity, Thais of all ages watch a traditional dance-comedy at Lak Muang, shrine of the city's guardian spirit.

This custom, performed to encourage the onset of rains, met with few complaints in the intense April heat and used to take place all over Bangkok. It is now banned lest drivers, blinded by water, lose control of their vehicles. All that happens in the city now is a ritual bathing of Buddha images and a ceremony in which young people respectfully trickle jasmine-scented water on to the hands of family elders, with a prayer for their happiness. Crowds of people therefore drive beyond the city limits to an area near the mouth of the Chao Phya River where water-throwing continues with traditional gusto, and where boat races, ritual tugs of war and processions of floats provide entertainment for everyone.

Festivals are not only unequalled in providing the most vital element of *sanuk*-ness—a huge crowd of happy people—but they also offer a *sabai* element of beauty. In this respect I always enjoy the fair held annually at Phra Chedi Klang Nam, the Sacred Tower in the Midst of the Waters—an island temple built by King Rama II a little way downriver from the city to house relics supposedly of the Buddha himself. For several nights in succession, this graceful temple with its tapering reliquary tower is floodlit; the lights of fair-booths and ferry boats along the banks of the Chao Phya River, reflected in its dancing waters, make a perfect setting for what is at once a religious rite and an occasion for pleasure. The crowds are so dense that the temporary parking area near the fairground extends for more than half a mile.

Gaily dressed families push their way through the narrow lanes among the booths and somehow gain a footing on one of the overcrowded ferries that will convey them to the island. A few moments of chugging across the river—which now looks like a black velvet band studded with myriads of diamond lights—brings them to the steps of the temple, where they leap or stumble ashore like pirates descending on a captive vessel. But here a hush falls. The people walk sedately to stalls where white-robed temple women dispense flowers, candles and incense sticks arranged in neat bundles, one for each person. Ascending a flight of stone steps to a gallery at the base of the reliquary tower where a statue of the Buddha stands, each worshipper finds enough room to squat on his haunches and make his offerings, murmuring words of homage and of aspiration for the happiness of all beings. Then he fixes his guttering candle to one of the spikes placed for the purpose in front of the statue, plants his smoking incense stick in a great bowl tightly packed with ash, and strews his flowers wherever there is space for them. But there is seldom room to complete his act of homage with the customary three prostrations; so, with joined palms raised to the forehead, the little ceremony is concluded. Now comes the time to go back across the river to the fairground—for the smooth blending of piety and lightheartedness is the essence of religious festivals.

The Festival of Floating Lights is another favourite excuse for general amusement—assuming, that is, one can reach the river's edge. Here people congregate to launch the frail craft called *krathong*, little lotus-shaped floats made of bamboo and leaves, coloured paper, or plastic. In the centre of each *krathong*, a candle and three incense sticks rise from a heap of flowers concealing one or two small coins. Squatting at the water's edge, their owners launch them with a murmured prayer and watch anxiously in the hope that they will float well away from the bank. Should they overturn, or should the candle be blown out quickly by the breeze, it means that the river deities will not allow their owners' misfortunes to be carried away; but if they float bravely off with the candle still burning, all will be well in the coming year. These days it is best, perhaps, to launch one's float on a smooth canal or pond, since the river is sure to be crowded with revellers in boats, and the wash overturns the *krathong* without care for the dashed hopes of the people who floated them.

One of the most popular festivals is the King's Birthday (December 5), when most of Bangkok is adorned with coloured light bulbs, flags, portraits of the monarch, and signs expressing wishes for the King's long life and happiness. Finally, on New Year's Eve, almost everyone goes out to *pai teeo*. Cinemas, restaurants and nightclubs are packed. On the Pramane Ground, thousands of milling citizens hail one another, whether friends or strangers, with shouted greetings. Suddenly, on the stroke of midnight, Brahman priests blow sacred conches. The crowds fall silent. The eerie sound, deemed holy and auspicious since remotest antiquity, is broadcast by radio and television to every corner of the city. It is like a solemn, long-drawn wailing. Buddhist monks begin a sonorous chant, and the New Year is ushered in by the words: "Homage to the Blessed One, the Holy One, the All-Enlightened", The people, surfeited with *pai teeo* and *sanuk*, pause to reflect upon what the coming year may hold. And well they might. For there is a touch of the miraculous about this capital of a land surrounded by potential enemies, yet keeping alive—for all its poverty and over-crowding—the spirit of delight. As to whether that spirit is now a flicker of wilful blindness, like dancing on the eve of battle, or whether it is a talisman for a stronger and happier future, the gods are silent.

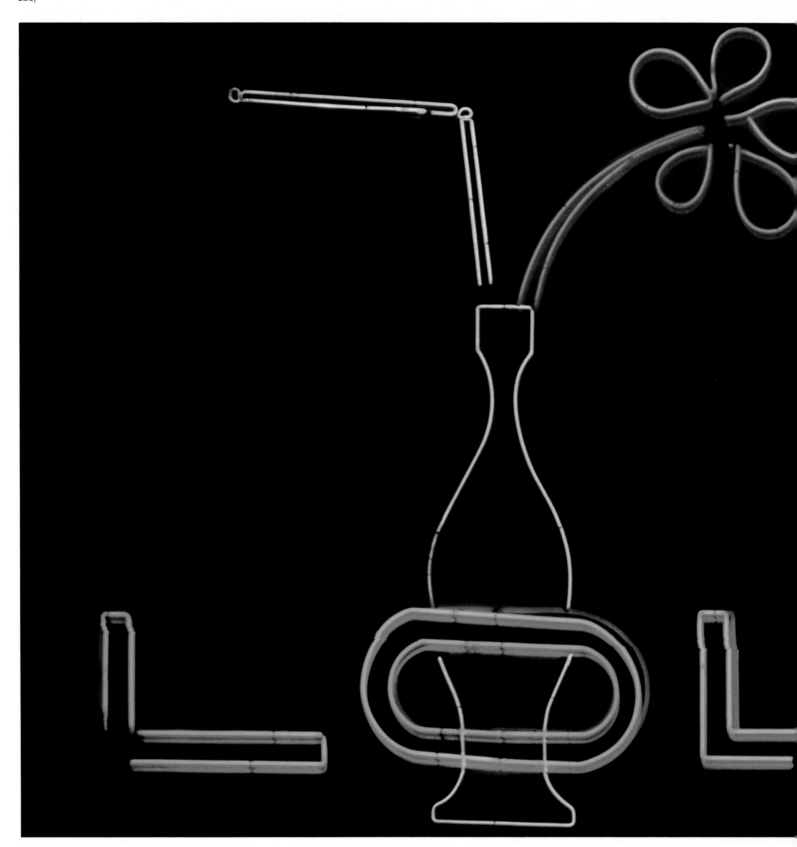

Neon Night-World

A sign outside a nightclub on Rajadamnoen Avenue recalls the influence of free-spending GIs who poured through Bangkok during the Vietnam War.

In the afterglow of the tropical sunset, Thailand's many-templed capital flickers to life in a second guise—as a neon-laced centre of night-life without peer in the East. The key workers of night-time Bangkok are an estimated 200,000 girls who have exchanged the drudgery of remote paddy-fields for careers as go-go dancers, bar hostesses, disco partners or prostitutes. Business is rarely slow, since Thai men love to gather in groups and venture forth to savour the night's various pleasures. Visiting foreigners provide another rich source of patronage, as did American soldiers when Bangkok was a rest and recreation centre during the Vietnam War. But no matter where or what the action, it is likely to have an unmistakably Thai flavour—a spontaneous warmth and graceful decorum that can lend dignity even to the sexual rituals of the massage parlours.

An illuminated spirit house, complete with a doll-like inmate representing a servant of the resident deity, stands in the luxuriant gardens of the Sing Thong (Golden Lion) restaurant. This popular outdoor night-spot offers powerfully amplified pop music by local entertainers, such as the booted balladeer with her group above.

Ten finalists in a beauty contest—a popular occasion for a social outing in Bangkok—exhibit their petite figures and winning smiles on a luxury hotel's stage.

As her distracted partner eyes a newcomer, a red-clad hostess at a dance-hall on New Petchburi Road demonstrates her skill at the latest Western-style dances

Bangkok's passion for pop music includes an Elvis Presley cult, exemplified by the long-running success of Visoot (insert), a local singer who impersonates the late star.

Perched on tiny stages above the bar, go-go dancers perform their vigorous routines at a Patpong Road night-spot, the "Mississippi River Queen". In the bars linin

is road and a parallel street dubbed Patpong II, the clientele—mainly tourists and foreign businessmen—buy drinks for the hostesses who keep them company.

In the foyer of a massage parlour, a customer smokes thoughtfully as he assesses the charms of girls ranged on tiers behind a two-way mirror and wearing numbers

eir blouses. The girls provide patrons with a hot bath and body massage in a private room—possibly followed, for an extra charge, by other "special services".

Bibliography

Audric, John, *Siam, Land of Temples.* Robert Hale Limited, London, 1962.

Basche, James, *Thailand, Land of the Free.* Taplinger Publishing Co. Inc., New York, 1971.

Blofeld, John, *King Maha Mongkut of Siam.* Asia Pacific Press, Singapore, 1972.

Blofeld, John, *People of the Sun.* Hutchinson, London, 1960.

Bowring, Sir John, *The Kingdom and People of Siam* (2 vols.). John W. Parker and Son, London, 1857.

Bruce, Helen, *Nine Temples of Bangkok.* Progress Book Store, Bangkok, 1960.

Bunnag, Jane, *Buddhist Monk, Buddhist Layman.* Cambridge University Press, London, 1973.

Caldwell, John C., *Massage Girl.* Robert Hale and Company, London, 1968.

Charnvit Kasetsiri, *The Rise of Ayudhya.* Oxford University Press, London, 1976.

Chula Chakrabongse, Prince, *Lords of Life.* Alvin Redman Limited, London, 1960.

Clarac, Achille, and Smithies, Michael, *Discovering Thailand.* Siam Publications Ltd., Bangkok, 1971.

Coughlin, R. J., *The Chinese in Bangkok.* University Microfilms, Inc., Michigan, 1969.

Coughlin, Richard J., *Double Identity, the Chinese in Modern Thailand.* Hong Kong University Press, Hong Kong, 1960.

Crawfurd, John, *Journal of an Embassy to the Courts of Siam and Cochin-China.* London, 1828.

Cripps, Francis, *The Far Province.* Hutchinson & Co. Ltd., London, 1965.

Crosby, Sir Josiah, *Siam: the Crossroads.* Hollis & Carter Ltd., London, 1945.

Dannhorn, Robin J., and Moore, Richard (eds.), *Fodor's South-East Asia 1978.* Hodder and Stoughton, London, 1978.

Darling, Frank and Ann, *Thailand, the Modern Kingdom.* Donald Moore for Asia Pacific Press, Singapore, 1971.

Davies, David M., *The Rice Bowl of Asia.* Robert Hale, London, 1967.

Davies, Derek A. C., *Thailand.* Kodansha International Ltd., Tokyo, 1970.

Donner, Wolf, *The Five Faces of Thailand.* C. Hurst & Co., London, 1978.

Duncan, William, *Thailand.* Charles E. Tuttle Company, Inc., Rutland, Vermont and Tokyo, 1976.

Fisher, Charles A., *South-east Asia.* Methuen & Co. Ltd., London, 1964.

Henderson, John W., and others, *Area Handbook for Thailand.* U.S. Government Printing Office, Washington D.C., 1971.

Humphreys, Christmas, *Buddhism.* Penguin Books, Harmondsworth, 1962.

Hutchinson, E. W., *Adventurers in Siam in the Seventeenth Century.* The Royal Asiatic Society, London, 1940.

Ingram, James C., *Economic Change in Thailand 1850-1970.* Stanford University Press, Stanford, 1971.

Insor, D., *Thailand.* George Allen and Unwin Ltd., London, 1963.

Kirkup, James, *Bangkok.* Phoenix House, London, 1968.

Kruger, Rayne, *The Devil's Discus.* Cassell & Co. Ltd., London, 1964.

Landon, Kenneth Perry, *Siam in Transition.* Oxford University Press, London, 1939.

Landon, Margaret, *Anna and the King of Siam.* George G. Harrap & Co. Ltd., London, 1945.

Leonowens, Anna, *The English Governess at the Siamese Court.* Arthur Barker Ltd., London, 1954.

Leonowens, Mrs. Anna H., *Siamese Harem Life.* Arthur Barker Ltd., London, 1952.

Levine, Charles (ed.), *Thailand.* APA Productions, Singapore and Hong Kong, 1977.

Ling, Trevor, *The Buddha.* Penguin Books, Harmondsworth, 1976.

McGee, T. G., *The Southeast Asian City.* G. Bell and Sons Ltd., London, 1967.

Manich Jumsai, M. L., *Thai Ramayana.* Chalermnit Press, Bangkok, 1977.

Manich Jumsai, M. L., *Understanding Thai Buddhism.* Chalermnit Press, Bangkok, 1971.

Mattani Rutnin (ed.), *The Siamese Theatre.* Collection of reprints from the Journals of the Siam Society, Bangkok, 1975.

Moffat, Abbot Low, *Mongkut, the King of Siam.* Cornell University Press, Ithaca, New York, 1961.

Moore, Frank J., *Thailand.* Hrof Press, New Haven, 1974.

Nagel Publishers, *Nagel's Encyclopedia-Guide Thailand Angkor (Cambodia).* Geneva, 1973.

The National Culture Institute, *Thailand Culture. Series 1-17.* Bangkok, 1953-54.

Neale, F. A., *Residence at the Capital of Siam.* Office of the National Illustrated Library, London, 1852.

Papineau, Aristide J. G. (ed.), *Papineau's Guide to Bangkok.* André Publications, Singapore, 1977.

Purcell, Victor, *The Chinese in Southeast Asia.* Oxford University Press, London, 1965.

Quaritch Wales, H. G., *Siamese State Ceremonies.* Bernard Quaritch Ltd., London, 1931.

Seidenfaden, Major Erik, *Guide to Bangkok.* The Royal State Railways of Siam, Bangkok, 1928.

Skinner, G. William, *Chinese Society in Thailand.* Cornell University Press, New York, 1957.

Smith, Malcolm, *A Physician at the Court of Siam.* Country Life Limited, London, 1947.

Spinks, Charles Nelson, *The Ceramic Wares of Siam.* The Siam Society, Bangkok, 1965.

Tambiah, S. J., *World Conqueror and World Renouncer.* Cambridge University Press, London, 1976.

Terwiel, B. J., *Monks and Magic.* Curzon Press, London, 1975.

Thompson, P. A., *Lotus Land.* T. Werner Laurie, London, 1906.

Ward, Barbara E., *Women in the New Asia.* UNESCO, Paris, 1963.

Warren, William, *Bangkok.* Weatherhill Serasia, New York, Tokyo and Hong Kong, 1972.

Waugh, Alec, *Bangkok.* W. H. Allen, London and New York, 1970.

Wells, Kenneth E., *Thai Buddhism.* Published by the author, 1960.

Wenk, Klaus, *The Restoration of Thailand under Rama I, 1782-1809.* The University of Arizona Press, Tucson, 1968.

Wood, W. A. R., *A History of Siam.* T. Fisher Unwin, Ltd., London, 1926.

Wray, Elizabeth, Rosenfield, Clare, and Bailey, Dorothy, *Ten Lives of the Buddha.* John Weatherhill, Inc., New York, 1972.

Young, Ernest, *The Kingdom of the Yellow Robe.* Archibald Constable & Co., London, 1900.

Acknowledgements and Picture Credits

The editors wish to thank the following for their valuable assistance: Dr. Manas Chitakasem, London; Domneun Garden, Bangkok; Heather Holden, London; David Lawton, Bangkok; Dr. Michael Leifer, London; Pradian Pecharak, Bangkok; the Svasti family, Bangkok; Hans Tasiemka, London; Thailand Information Service, London; Giles Wordsworth, London.

Sources for pictures in this book are shown below. Credits for the pictures from left to right are separated by commas; from top to bottom by dashes.

All photographs are by Philip Jones Griffiths except: Pages 16, 17—Map by Hunting Surveys Ltd., London (Silhouettes by Norman Bancroft-Hunt, Caterham Hill, Surrey). 85—Biblioteca Apostolica Vaticana, Rome. 86, 87—Radio Times Hulton Picture Library. 89—David L. Terry. 91—Popperfoto. 92—Philip Jones Griffiths from Magnum Photos. 143—David Brinson.

Index

Numerals in italics indicate a photograph or drawing of the subject mentioned.

Colour reproduction by Irwin Photography Ltd., at their Leeds Studio.
Filmsetting by C. E. Dawkins (Typesetters) Ltd., London, SE1 1UN.
Printed and bound in Italy by Arnoldo Mondadori, Verona.